DR. BOB KENNETH

Money seed of Happiness

Cultivating Financial Independence and Abundance for a Happy Retirement

First edition

This book was professionally typeset on Reedsy.
Find out more at *reedsy.com*

Contents

1

Introduction

Cultivating Financial Independence and Abundance for a Money Seed of Happiness: Cultivating Financial Independence and Abundance for a Happy Retirement" is a ground-breaking literary work that goes beyond the traditional confines of financial self-help books. Dr. Bob Kenneth takes readers on an instructive tour into the complicated garden of personal finance, where the seed of monetary wisdom are sowed to reap an abundant harvest of happiness after retirement.

This book shines as a beacon of hope and empowerment in an era when financial security and contentment in retirement are becoming increasingly unattainable. Dr. Bob Kenneth provides readers with a compass to navigate the often stormy waters of personal finance with confidence and elegance, drawing on a wealth of knowledge gained through years of research and practical experience.

As readers explore the vast terrain of financial concepts, methods, and habits, the book's story unfolds like a horticulture expedition. Each chapter acts as a rich environment for the development of important financial abilities ranging from budgeting and investing to retirement planning and wealth protection. With each page turn, readers gain essential ideas that lay the groundwork for a profitable and fulfilling retirement.

The emphasis on the junction between financial plenty and emotional well-being distinguishes "Money Seeds of Happiness." Dr. Bob Kenneth recognizes that true happiness transcends mere wealth and works to empower readers to achieve not only financial independence but also a profound feeling of purpose and pleasure in retirement.

As readers progress through the book, they will come across real-life success stories, practical exercises, and thought-provoking thoughts that will inspire them to plant their own money seeds. Dr. Bob Kenneth expertly combines financial knowledge with a human tale, making complicated financial ideas understandable to readers of all backgrounds.

"Money Seed of Happiness" emerges as a timeless guide that transcends generations in a society where financial literacy is a key life skill. It is a road plan to not only financial independence but also a joyful retirement full of happiness, purpose, and wealth. So, embark on this life-changing journey, sow your money seeds, and watch them grow into a life of financial security and enduring delight.

2

Putting the Foundation in Place

Essentials of Speculation

The term "investment basics" refers to the main ideas and regulations that people should understand when it comes to saving money.

Key concepts and words to help you understand the principles of financial planning:

Speculations:

Speculations indicate danger, which alludes to the possibility of misfortune or unpredictability in the value of your undertaking. bigger-risk speculations, on average, have the potential for bigger rewards, whereas lower-risk ventures often provide lesser returns. It is critical to assess your wager in order to avoid the conflict between risk and prospective profits while making investment decisions.

Broadening your endeavor:

Broadening your endeavor means extending it across different resource classes (such as stocks, bonds, and land) and within each resource class (different enterprises, places, or organizations). Enhancement reduces the impact of a single speculating display on your overall portfolio. It can reduce risk while increasing the possibility of consistent profits.

Resource allocation:

Resource allocation refers to the distribution of your venture portfolio among several resource classifications. It entails selecting how much of your portfolio should be allocated to stocks, bonds, cash, and other investments. Resource allocation decisions are frequently based on characteristics such as your investment objectives, risk tolerance, and time horizon.

Time horizon:

Your time horizon is the amount of time you anticipate to hold an enterprise before requiring the assets. It can range from the present instant (less than a year) to the long term (a long time or more). Your time horizon influences your venture decisions, as longer time horizons may represent more prominent receptivity to potentially greater-risk guesses with the expectation of higher profits.

There are various speculating vehicles available, such as stocks, securities, pooled reserves, trade exchange reserves, land, and items, and that's just the tip of the iceberg. Every venture vehicle has unique characteristics, risks, and potential returns. Before making any financial decisions, it is vital to investigate and understand the features and components of numerous speculation vehicles.

Speculation returns:

Venture returns measure the profit or loss on a venture over a specific time period. Returns can be expressed as a percentage or as an absolute dollar value. Capital appreciation (growth in the value of the investment) and compensation (profits, interest, and rental pay) are typical proportions of venture returns.

Compounding:

Intensifying refers to a business's ability to generate income that is reinvested to generate additional profit. Compounding can have a significant impact on the devel of hypotheses over time. You can profit from both your underlying speculation and any accumulated gains by reinvesting returns.

Risk assessment:

Prior to investing, it is critical to assess your gambling tolerance. Risk resilience refers to an individual's enthusiasm and capacity to confront risk challenges in their speculations. Financial goals, time horizons, and individual circumstances all have an impact on risk resilience. To avoid experiencing extravagant risk obstacles and missing out on potential profits, you must tailor your venture choices to your gambling resistance.

Research and a reasonable degree of effort:

When exploring business opportunities, legitimate investigation and an acceptable amount of investment are essential. It entails obtaining data regarding ventures, such as checking fiscal reports, recognizing industry patterns, evaluating supervisory groups, and taking into account financial and economic problems. Careful investigation can help you make informed speculative judgments.

Speculation aims:

It is critical to define specific venture objectives. Objectives might be short-term (e.g., saving for a vacation), medium-term (e.g., buying a house), or long-term (e.g., retirement). Your objectives will determine your endeavor strategy, resource allocation, and time frame.

Remember that contributing can be difficult, and it's always a good idea to consult with a financial advisor or conduct extensive research before making business decisions.

The Center Standards' Danger and Prize Chance and prize are important rules that play an important role in many aspects of life, including business, finance, financial planning, navigation, and self-awareness. Understanding these criteria is critical for making educated judgments and moving forward. Let's look into the center's hazard and award standards:

Chance and Return Relationship:

The law of hazard and return indicates that higher degrees of chance are generally associated with the possibility for higher payouts. As a result, the more the risk an individual or organization takes, the greater the potential reward they can expect. This benchmark assists leaders in analyzing the trade-off between risk and reward and in determining the degree of risk they will tolerate in order to achieve their desired goals.

Risk Assessment:

Before embarking on any undertaking, it is critical to assess the risks involved. Recognizing and breaking down projected gambles, assessing their potential impact, and determining

7

the probability of their occurrence are all part of risk appraisal. Understanding the risks allows people and organizations to make informed decisions and go to appropriate lengths to monitor or mitigate the risks.

Expansion:

Expansion is a risk in the executive's process that involves extending guesses or exercises across multiple resources, businesses, or markets. People or organizations can reduce the overall risk of their portfolios or activities by growing. If one speculation or location fails to meet expectations or faces significant risks, the losses can be offset by the display of other endeavors or territories. Expansion strategies aim to achieve a balance between chance and prize by minimizing the impact of any single negative event.

Danger Craving:

Hazard hunger refers to a person's or organization's ability to recognize and bear danger. It varies from person to person and is influenced by factors such as financial constraints, goals, time frame, and risk tolerance. A select persons or organizations may have a stronger gambling need and will confront more serious dangers and hurdles in their pursuit of larger jackpots. Others may be less susceptible to craving and prefer more moderate approaches. Understanding one's gambling addiction is critical for modifying speculating tactics, dynamic cycles, and goals.

Risk The board:

Hazard the executives involves identifying, surveying, and mitigating risks in order to protect people or organizations from potential harm or loss. A continuous interaction includes risk identification, risk investigation, risk assessment, and risk mitigation methods. A powerful gamble the executives enables individuals and organizations to proactively manage anticipated risks and mitigate their impact. It ensures a balance between obtaining remuneration and defending against potential calamities.

Hazard and award are essential considerations in dynamic cycles. People or organizations analyze the potential risks and rewards of several options while simply deciding. This evaluation supports them in weighing predicted benefits against potential setbacks and making informed decisions. Chiefs should consider the potential consequences of their decisions, examine the risk-reward trade-off, and tailor their judgments to their overall goals and risk tolerance.

Continuous Learning and Transformation:

Hazard and reward criteria necessitate continuous learning, variation, and evaluation. Markets, conditions, and conditions change throughout time, which might have an impact on the gamble and award parts. To investigate effectively, people and organizations must stay refreshed, screen patterns, collect important data, and adapt their approaches accordingly. Profiting from both victories and defeats concerns the refining of chance administration and the simplification of the gamble reward balance.

It is critical to remember that gambling and winnings are inextricably linked but inherently uncertain. What is to come is unusual, and there are no guarantees of clear outcomes. People and organizations should continue to survey gambles, extend their approaches, and use appropriate gamble administration processes to improve their genuine capability for remuneration while avoiding potential downsides.

Commonly used venture wordings that made sense in simple terms:

A stock is a type of ownership interest in a company. When you buy a stock, you become an investor with a claim on the company's wealth and earnings.

A security is a type of obligation speculation in which you loan money to an organization or government in exchange for regular premium installments and the arrival of the principal sum at growth.

A common asset is a speculative vehicle that pools money from numerous financial supporters to put resources into a distinct arrangement of stocks, bonds, or other assets.

A file reserve is a type of common asset or trade traded store that reproduces the exhibition of a certain market record, such as the S&P 500. It provides broad market access and is due.

Expansion:
To reduce risk, diversify your ventures among numerous resources (e.g., stocks, bonds, land) and fields (e.g., innovation, medical services). It aids in avoiding concentrating your resources in one location.

Profit from Speculation (return on investment):

The return on original capital investment measures a venture's productivity. It is the rate of increase or decrease in the value of speculation over a specific time period, taking into account both capital additions and pay produced.

Risk refers to the possibility of tragedy or unpredictability in speculation returns. Various projects carry varying levels of risk, with greater-risk speculations generally having the possibility for higher returns.

Profit:
A profit is a payment made by an organization to its investors, usually in the form of money or more offerings. It addresses a portion of the benefits distributed to the proprietors by the organization.

A capital increase is a benefit recognized from selling speculation at a higher cost than the initial price tag. It occurs when the selling price exceeds the expense premise.

Resource Allotment:
Resource allocation is the process of dividing enterprises among several resource classes (e.g., stocks, bonds, cash) based on a financial backer's objectives, risk tolerance, and time horizon.

Buyer Market:
A buyer market is characterized by growing stock prices and financial backers' confidence. It is characterized by increased demands and good financial backer attitudes.

Bear Market:

A bear market is characterized by decreasing stock prices and investor negativity. It is characterized by waning interest and bad financial supporter attitudes.

Remember that these clarifications are condensed, and contributing involves complexities beyond these concepts. Before making any speculative decisions, it is critical to conduct thorough research or get professional advice.

3

The Mindset of a Financial Backer

The Mindset of a Financial Backer

Fostering a successful financial backer mindset is critical for exploring the prospective and less promising times of the monetary company sectors and making sensible speculation choices.

Consider the following important issues:

Instructions and details:

Contributing is an adventure that necessitates continuous learning. Make time to educate yourself on distinct venture methods, resource classes, and monetary concepts. Keep up to date on market trends, financial indicators, and industry news. The more knowledge you obtain, the better prepared you will be to make smart business decisions.

Long-term perspective:

Profitable financial supporters recognize the necessity of

adopting a long view. They believe that market fluctuations are crucial for the contributing system and focus on the overall direction of their guesses. By adopting a long-term mindset, you can brave market volatility while potentially benefiting from the intensifying impact of profits in the long run.

The board of risk:

Risk management is a fundamental component of effective money management. Understand your gambling resilience, which refers to your ability to withstand fluctuations in the value of your bets. Diversify your portfolio over several resource classes and areas to mitigate the impact of any single speculation. Audit and rebalance your portfolio on a regular basis to ensure that it aligns with your risk profile and business objectives.

Discipline and tolerance:

To contribute, tolerance and discipline are required. Effective financial backers avoid making rash decisions based on short-term market changes or emotions. They stick to their trading strategy and resist the urge to time the market. All else being equal, they focus on their long-term goals and stick to their money-growth approach even during difficult circumstances.

Accepting Vulnerability:

The financial business sectors are inherently volatile, and vulnerability is critical for the contributing landscape. Effective financial backers accept vulnerability and recognize that they

14

have no control over or ability to predict every market move. Overall, they focus on elements under their control, such as resource allocation, expansion, and risk management. They also maintain a rational perspective and have backup plans in place for various market circumstances.

Getting a Glimpse of the Board:

Feelings might stymie speculating success. Beneficial financial backers are aware of their emotions and strive to make sound decisions based on extensive research and investigation. They try not to make business judgments based solely on fear or avarice. They can maintain a more objective and sensible approach to financial planning by keeping their emotions under control.

Continuous Evaluation and Transformation:

The speculative scene is fluid, with effective financial supporters adapting to shifting economic conditions. Evaluate your trading system, portfolio execution, and financial goals on a regular basis. Be prepared to adapt your process if necessary due to new facts or changes in the market conditions.

Looking for Effective Advice:

Consider seeking professional advice from financial advisors or investment specialists. They can provide advice that is specific to your financial situation and goals. A reputable consultant can provide valuable information, assist you in researching complex business options, and provide an objective viewpoint.

Remember that cultivating a profitable financial supporter mindset requires time and experience. Show self-control and accept learning valuable open doors along the way. You may boost your chances of achieving your investment objectives and establishing long-term wealth by cultivating the proper mindset.

Normal business Terms

Stock:

In an organization, a stock addresses possession. When you buy a stock, you become an investor with a claim on the organization's resources and profits.

Security:

A security is a type of obligation speculation in which you lend money to a company or government in exchange for regular premium installments and the arrival of the principal sum at maturity.

Common Property:

A shared asset is a venture vehicle that pools funds from numerous investors to invest in a diverse portfolio of stocks, bonds, or other securities.

List of Assets:

A file reserve is a type of shared asset or trading exchange store that aims to replicate the display of a certain market record, such as the S&P 500. It provides broad market openness and is passively made due.

Broadening:

To reduce risk, diversify your bets among numerous resources (e.g., stocks, bonds, land) and areas (e.g., innovation, medical treatment). It aids in avoiding tying up your valuables in one location.

Speculation Profit (return on investment):

The return on capital invested evaluates a company's productivity. It is the rate of increase or decrease in the value of a venture over a specific time period, taking into account both capital additions and pay generated.

Risk:

The term "hazard" refers to the possibility of disaster or unpredictability in speculating returns. Various projects have varying amounts of risk, with greater-risk speculations generally contributing to the possibility for bigger returns.

Profit:

A profit is a payment given by an organization to its investors, usually in the form of money or additional offers. It covers a portion of the benefits communicated to the owners by the organization.

Increase in capital:

A capital addition is a benefit recognized from selling a business at a higher price than the initial cost. It occurs when the selling price exceeds the expense premise.

Portion of resources:

The technique of dividing endeavors across numerous resource classes (e.g., equities, bonds, cash) according on a financial backer's objectives, risk tolerance, and time horizon.

Market for Buyers:

A rising market is characterized by growing stock prices and trust among financial supporters. It is characterized by increased demands and good financial backer attitudes.

The Bear Market:

A bear market is characterized by decreasing stock prices and investor pessimism. It is characterized by waning enthusiasm and negative financial backer sentiment.

Remember that these clarifications are condensed, and contributing involves complexities beyond these concepts. Before embarking on any enterprise, it is critical to conduct thorough research or seek professional advice.

Creating an Effective Financial Supporter Outlook

Contributing may be both exciting and challenging. Fostering an effective financial supporter mindset is vital for exploring the hopeful and less promising periods of the monetary business sectors and making smart speculation decisions.

Important considerations include:

Instructions and details:

Contributing is an adventure that necessitates continuous learning. Make time to educate yourself on various business practices, resource classes, and financial concepts. Keep up to date on market trends, financial indicators, and industry news. The more knowledge you obtain, the better prepared you will be to make educated speculative decisions.

Long-term Perspective:

Effective financial backers recognize the necessity of adopting a long view. They believe that temporary market fluctuations are crucial for the contributing system and place emphasis on the general direction of their speculations. By adopting a patient mindset, you can brave market volatility and perhaps benefit from the intensifying impact of profits over time.

The board of risk:

Risk management is a fundamental component of effective money management. Understand your gambling resilience, which refers to your ability to withstand fluctuations in the value of your bets. Increase the diversity of your portfolio across several resource classes and areas to reduce the impact of any particular initiative. Audit and rebalance your portfolio on a regular basis to ensure that it matches your risk tolerance and investment objectives.

Discipline and perseverance:

Contributing necessitates perseverance and discipline. Successful financial backers avoid making rash decisions based on fleeting market devels or emotions. They stick to their business plan and resist the urge to time the market. Overall, they focus on their long-term goals and remain committed to their money-growth strategy, even during difficult times.

Accepting Vulnerability:

The financial business sectors are inherently volatile, and vulnerability is critical for the contributing scene. Effective financial backers accept vulnerability and recognize that they cannot control or predict every market variation. Overall, they focus on factors within their control, such as resource allocation, expansion, and executive risks. They also maintain a reasonable perspective and have backup plans in place for various market situations.

Getting a Glimpse of the Board:

Feelings can stymie business success. Profitable financial backers are aware of their emotions and strive to make rational decisions based on extensive research and investigation. They try not to make business decisions based solely on fear or hunger. By keeping feelings within appropriate boundaries, they can maintain a more goal-oriented and consistent approach to financial planning.

Continuous Evaluation and Transformation:

The speculative scene is fluid, with effective financial supporters adapting to shifting economic conditions. Evaluate your trading system, portfolio execution, and financial goals on a regular basis. Be willing to change your methodology if new data or changes in the market climate require it.

Looking for Skilled Counsel:

Consider seeking professional advice from financial advisors or venture experts. They can provide advice that is specific to your financial situation and goals. A trusted consultant can provide valuable information, assist you in researching complex business options, and provide an objective viewpoint.

Keep in mind that developing an effective financial backer mindset requires time and practice. Show self-control and accept learning valuable open doors along the way. You can improve your chances, achieve your investment goals, and build long-term financial security by cultivating the appropriate mindset.

Overcoming Deep Predispositions in Financial Planning

Feelings play a significant role in our decisions, including smart financial planning. Deep inclinations can impair judgment and lead to rash business judgments. However, by comprehending these tendencies and putting in place procedures to counteract them, financial backers can make more rational and informed decisions.

Few Common deep tendencies and how to overcome them:

Preference for predictable solutions:
   The tendency to seek predictable solutions is the tendency to seek data that confirms our present beliefs while disregarding or discounting conflicting evidence. To overcome the temptation to seek out predefined comments, successfully seek out other ideas and consider alternative perspectives. Participate in extensive exploration and examination, putting your assumptions and convictions to the test. Accept data that questions your basic assumptions, since it might lead to a more appropriate and objective course of action.

Misfortune Abhorrence:
   Misfortune abhorrence alludes to the inclination to experience the aggravation of misfortunes more firmly than the delight of riches. This impulse can cause financial backers to clutch losing speculations for a long period or remain away from essential

22

portfolio alterations. To battle disaster abhorrence, center around the drawn-out execution of your portfolio instead of temporary modifications. Set obvious stop-misfortune constraints or foreordained leave objectives to assist with overseeing disadvantage danger. Moreover, continuously assess your portfolio to ensure it lines up with your speculation objectives and hazard resistance.

Group Attitude:

Group attitude develops when people follow the activities and choices of the bigger part, it is legitimate to expect that the aggregate insight. This inclination can induce exaggerated or underestimated ventures because of market air pockets or frenzies. To counter the crowd mindset, lead solo exploration and investigation. Pursue speculation selections in light of your assessment of vital factors as opposed to aimlessly following the group. Consider the drawn-out suitability of an enterprise as opposed to momentary market sensation.

Arrogance:

Arrogance tendency encourages financial backers to have an outrageous conviction in their power to forecast market events or outflank the market reliably. To fight presumptuousness, have a modest and sensible outlook. Consider that contributing implies vulnerability, and that even seasoned specialists cannot predict the market with certainty. Differentiate your endeavors, use a trained speculation technique, and constantly evaluate and profit from your speculation selections.

Predisposition to Mooring:

Mooring tendency occurs when financial backers rely heavily on the underlying snippet of data they obtain while deciding, regardless of whether it is currently irrelevant. To overcome the mooring bias, gather a wide range of evidence and opinions before making speculating decisions. Constantly examine your speculation hypothesis and be willing to adjust your approach in response to fresh data and changing economic conditions. Try not to become overly attached to specific value targets or preliminary speculating assumptions.

Predisposition to Recency:

Recency bias refers to the tendency to prioritize recent events or performance while making business decisions. To overcome the recency bias, take a step back and consider the verified execution and basics of supposition. Try not to base automatic replies solely on transient market fluctuations. Instead than focusing on little modifications, concentrate on the overall pattern and underlying value of the venture.

Separation: close to home

Separation close to home is critical in combating profound predispositions. While making business decisions, use attention and mindfulness to assess your immediate surroundings. Take breaks from constantly examining your portfolio to avoid becoming overwhelmed by fleeting market fluctuations. Consider establishing clear venture guidelines and strategies in advance to guide your dynamic cycle.

Remember that overcoming close-to-home money management tendencies is a never-ending cycle. By monitoring these
tendencies and implementing mechanisms to balance them,
you may refine your strategy and increase the likelihood of
long-term venture success. Furthermore, seeking advice from
financial specialists can provide an objective point of view and
assist you in addressing personal issues in successful money
management.

Effective Financial Planning: The Brain Science

Contributing isn't just about data, graphs, and financial analysis.
Human brain research has also had a significant impact. Understanding the mental components of efficient financial planning
can help financial backers make more informed decisions and
investigate market highs and lows. Here are some essential
mental factors to consider:

Insight into Risk:
  People encounter and endure risk in unexpected ways. Some
financial backers are more risk-averse, preferring more secure
and mild speculations, whereas others are more risk-tolerant,
seeking higher returns through less secure enterprises. Understanding your risk tolerance is critical for tailoring your
endeavor selections to your degree of comfort. It is critical to
recognize that risk assessment might fluctuate as a result of
factors such as economic conditions, individual circumstances,
and late venture encounters.

Conduct Preferences:

Social inclinations are intrinsic mental proclivities that might influence business strategy. Normal predispositions contain a proclivity to seek predictable feedback (searching for evidence that confirms current convictions), securing proclivity (relying heavily on starting data), and loss aversion (feeling the agony of losses more strongly than the delight of gains). Perceiving these tendencies and effectively seeking to control them can lead to more rational business decisions.

Mindset in a Group:

People have a natural tendency to mimic the behaviors and choices of the majority, therefore it is reasonable to assume aggregate understanding. This crowd mentality can result in venture air pockets or frenzies, since financial backers will frequently pursue directions rather than guiding unfettered research. Monitoring crowd attitudes and making business decisions based on individual examination and investigation can help to avoid irrational speculative behaviors.

Pomposity:

Pomposity propensity causes financial backers to have un-reasonable trust in their ability to predict market movements or consistently outperform the market. This proclivity might lead to expensive trading, speculative endeavors, or risk mis-judgment. Fighting presumptuousness entails maintaining a practical perspective, acknowledging the inherent weakness in efficient financial planning, and focusing on concentrated

26

speculating approaches rather than relying on premonitions or hunches.

Localized Effects:

Feelings can have a significant impact on business decisions. Fear and insatiability are powerful emotions that might lead financial backers to make rash decisions. During market downturns, fear can lead to panic selling, whereas voracity can lead to the pursuit of high-flying businesses without a legitimate reasonable degree of effort. Dealing with sentiments entails recognizing the significant impact on course, returning to a previous stage to fairly examine options, and taking into consideration the long-term perspective.

Market Prediction:

Many financial backers attempt to time the market, anticipating the finest times to trade speculations. However, market timing is notoriously difficult, even if it is certainly possible to accomplish consistently. According to research, timing the market is rarely profitable in the long run. Taking on a trained venture strategy, focusing on long-term aims, and avoiding reactive decisions based on temporary market variances will normally yield better results.

Discipline and perseverance:

Persistence and discipline are essential mental traits for successful financial planning. Contributing is a long-term endeavor, and the ability to stay focused on long-term goals while resisting indiscreet choices is essential. Avoiding risky trading, maintaining a well-diversified portfolio, and adhering to a predetermined growth strategy can all help to develop tenacity and discipline.

Learning and adaptability:

Contributing is a never-ending learning journey. Maintaining an open mind to new data, market developments, and altering procedures as needed is critical for long-term success. Investors should evaluate and learn from previous venture decisions, including successes and failures, and adjust their strategy as needed.

Understanding the cognitive science of financial planning can improve the dynamic cycle of a financial backer. Financial backers can seek more sane and informed decisions by monitoring mental predispositions, managing with feelings, and maintaining discipline. Seeking advice from financial specialists can also provide an impartial perspective and aid in the exploration of the mental challenges inherent in effective financial planning.

4

Vehicles of Speculation

Stocks: The Building Blocks of Wealth

Stocks play an important role as the building blocks of abundance in the world of good money management. When you acquire stocks, you become a fractional owner of a company, allowing you the opportunity to participate in its growth and gain.

Understanding stocks and their role in financial stability:

Possession and Profitability:

When you purchase stock, you are getting a piece of the organization's proprietorship. As an investor, you can benefit from the company's success through capital appreciation and profits. If the organization does well, the value of your parts may rise over time, allowing you to sell them at a higher price. Furthermore, some businesses distribute a portion of their revenues to investors, providing a consistent revenue stream.

Enhancement and Opportunity Management:

Stocks enable investors to diversify their investments. You can spread your risk and reduce the impact of any single initiative by putting resources into stocks across multiple firms and enterprises. Expansion protects your wealth against the possible demise of a certain organization or area. While expanding your stock portfolio, it is vital to consider your risk tolerance and speculation goals.

Long-term Development Prospects:

Stocks have generally demonstrated long-term development potential. While the stock market can be unpredictable in the short term, it has consistently demonstrated vertical patterns over the long term. Patient financial backers who invested in the market have often been compensated for their long-term commitment. The multiplier effect of reinvesting revenues and allowing your businesses to grow over time can significantly contribute to financial stability.

Data and Market Productivity:

The securities market is well-known for its ability to accurately represent publicly available data. The expenses of collective operations and the views of millions of financial backers are still up in the air. As a result, it may be attempting to consistently outflank the market. However, persistent examination, critical research, and being up to date on the organization's financial well-being and industry patterns will help you make sound business decisions.

Venture Methods:

Investing in equities provides a variety of venture approaches to meet diverse inclinations and aims. A few financial backers use an uninvolved methodology by investing in file assets or trade traded reserves (ETFs) that monitor a specific market record. This approach provides broad market access and, for the most part, inexpensive costs. Others prefer a working process in which they select particular equities based on their research and analysis. Dynamic money management involves more commitment, effort, and skill, but also has the potential for higher returns.

Effective Direction:

Investing in stocks can be difficult, especially for individuals who are new to the market. Seeking professional guidance from financial advisors or venture experts can provide valuable information and assist you in navigating the complexity of stock money management. They can assist you in assessing your risk tolerance, laying down practical assumptions, and developing a venture process that is in line with your financial objectives.

It is critical to remember that investing in equities involves risks, including the possibility of capital loss. Stock prices can be volatile and influenced by a variety of factors, including monetary conditions, organizational execution, and market sentiment. As a result, it is critical to thoroughly investigate and examine your speculative options.

Stocks, in general, operate as structural blocks of abundance by providing opportunities for long-term development and abundant collection. Stocks can be a valuable instrument for developing financial momentum and meeting financial goals with careful planning, research, and knowledgeable navigation.

Fixed-Pay Speculations and Bonds

Bonds and fixed-pay speculations are well-known financial assets that provide stability and pay to investors. These speculations provide a predictable stream of payments and are regarded less risky than stocks. This is what you should be aware of while investing in bonds and fixed-income securities:

What exactly are bonds?

Securities are obligation protections provided by legislatures, districts, and corporations in order to raise funds. When you purchase a security, you are making a loan to the backer for a set length of time. As a result, the backer promises to pay you a premium at a predetermined rate (coupon rate) and refund the principal money at development.

Capital Preservation and Solidity:

Bonds are well-known for their durability and ability to conserve capital. They are generally seen as less volatile than equities, giving them an appealing option for modest or pay-focused financial backers. Bonds have a respectable revenue stream, making them a vital component of a diversified speculative portfolio.

Bonds of several types:

There are various types of securities available, such as government securities, corporate securities, municipal securities, and depository securities. Government securities are issued by public legislatures, whilst municipal bonds are issued by state and local government administrations. Organizations issue corporate securities to raise funds for a variety of reasons. Depository bonds are issued by the government and are among the most secure bond investments.

Pay Age and Yield:

The yield on a securities is the yearly return that a financial backer can expect from the asset after accounting for its cost, coupon rate, and time to maturity. Bond coupon payments turn out to be a predictable revenue stream. Bond investors usually rely on this payment for regular income. Furthermore, some securities provide expense benefits, such as duty-free interest on civil bonds.

Chance of financing cost:

One important consideration when investing in securities is financing cost risk. Loan fees and security costs have an inverse connection. When lending fees rise, the costs of existing bonds typically fall. This occurs as new assets with higher financing costs become more appealing to financial investors. Alternatively, as interest rates fall, the value of existing bonds rises. Understanding loan cost trends is crucial when investing in bonds.

Credit Risk:

Another risk associated with bonds is credit risk. This refers to the possibility that the guarantor will fail to pay its installments, which include both interest and principal. Bonds with better credit ratings are considered safer since they are less likely to default. Financial backers regularly use ratings from organizations such as Moody's or Standard & Poor's to examine the dependability of bond guarantors.

Expansion and Resource Share:

Remembering bonds and fixed-pay initiatives for an improved portfolio can help to reduce overall portfolio risk. Securities, as opposed to equities, typically exhibit lower unpredictability, acting as a cradle during market downturns. Individual gamble resilience, venture targets, and time horizon all influence the best bond assignment. Offsetting bonds with other resource classes, such as stocks and money reciprocals, are common in resource portion systems.

Effective Exhortation:

Investing in bonds necessitates a thorough understanding of its benefits and drawbacks. Consider seeking advice from financial advisors or security professionals who can aid you in investigating the security market, assessing credit opportunities, and picking acceptable fixed-pay speculations. They can also assist you in developing a bond portfolio that aligns with your investment objectives and risk tolerance.

Bonds and fixed-pay projects provide financial backers with strength and pay. They provide predictable income, capital protection, and growth opportunities. Financial backers can employ securities to better their overall venture method by understanding the various types of securities, analyzing risks, and considering their role in the resource component.

Land: Significant Advantages

The land is a significant resource class that provides financial supporters with the opportunity to generate rewards through various ways. Whether for individual residences, company constructions, or land projects, land can provide enticing returns and a wide range of benefits. Here's a closer look at the potential benefits and drawbacks of investing in land:

Rental Payment:

One of the most important methods to profit from land is through rental payments. Financial supporters can generate a steady stream of income by purchasing and renting out homes. Private properties, such as lofts or single-family houses, can be leased to individuals, whereas commercial properties, such as office spaces or retail sites, can be rented to organizations. Rental income is a consistent source of money and can be a large source of automated revenue.

Appreciation:

Land provides the potential for long-term value appreciation. Over time, properties in favorable places will generally increase in value due to factors such as population growth, metropolitan transformation, and land scarcity. Financial supporters who hold properties for the long haul can profit from capital apprecia- tion, allowing them to sell the property at a higher price than the initial purchase price. Appreciation can fundamentally increase wealth accumulation and provide big gains from speculating.

Reduced taxes:

Land initiatives have a few duty advantages that can boost output. Rental pay is typically levied at preferential rates when compared to other types of remuneration. Financial backers can also profit from derivations such as contract revenue, municipal levies, and devaluation, which can reduce available pay and increase profits. Furthermore, when selling a venture property, investors may be eligible for tax benefits such as 1031 transactions, which contemplate charge-free reinvestment of proceeds into another property.

Upgrades and redesigns can help investors increase the value of their land investments. Financial supporters can attract more profitable occupants or increase resale esteem by improving the property's highlights, usefulness, or feel. Remodeling, organizing, or energy-efficient modifications can support rental pay and overall home appreciation.

Expansion Barrier:

Land speculation can operate as a barrier to expansion. When the economy expands, the value of properties and rental rates often rise, allowing investors to maintain purchasing power and possibly raise rental income. As the average cost of numerous ordinary things rises, rental rates can rise in tandem, resulting in a constant revenue stream that keeps pace with the rise.

It's important to remember that land-efficient money management entails risks and necessitates a careful expected level of investment. Economic situations, geography, property, executives, and finance arrangements, for example, can all have an impact on the benefit of land speculation. Working with skilled specialists, directing careful exploration, and understanding local land components can all help to reduce risks and increase the likelihood of positive outcomes.

In summary, the land provides undeniable benefits and a wide range of rewards to financial investors. Rent, property appreciation, tax breaks, impact, enhancement, and esteem-added upgrades

Shared assets and exchange-traded funds (ETFs)

Common assets and trade traded reserves (ETFs) are well-known investment instruments that give consumers access to a broad variety of protections. They provide advantages such as growth, competent administration, and flexibility.

list of common assets and ETFs:

Shared Resources:

Structure:
Shared reserves aggregate monies from several financial backers to invest in a portfolio of stocks, bonds, or other assets. They are governed by knowledgeable asset administrators who make investment decisions in the best interests of the financial backers. Financial supporters purchase shares in the common asset, and the asset's net resource worth accounts for the value of each offer.

Enhancement:
Expansion is one of the most important benefits of shared reserves. By investing in a common asset, financial backers receive access to a broad range of safeguards across multiple resource classes, initiatives, and geographic areas. This broadening reduces the risk associated with investing in particular equities or bonds.

Administration Skills:

Common assets are managed by qualified professionals who lead exploration, analyze market patterns, and make business decisions based on the asset's speculating aims. The capacity of the asset chief can be especially beneficial for financial backers who may lack the opportunity, information, or assets to efficiently manage their initiatives.

Various Venture Methodologies:
Shared reserves provide a wide range of speculating approaches to satisfy various financial backer preferences and objectives. There is value support that concentrates on stocks, fixed-pay finances that invest in securities, adjusted reserves that combine stocks and securities, record subsidies that track explicit market files, and area explicit assets that concentrate on unambiguous ventures.

Liquidity:
Common assets provide financial supporters with liquidity, which means they can exchange shares at the current NAV at any time. As a result, shared reserves are an advantageous solution for financial backers who require quick access to their speculating capital.

ETFs (Exchange Traded Funds):
Structure:
ETFs, like traditional investments, pool money from numerous financial backers. ETFs, on the other hand, are traded on stock exchanges in the same way that individual stocks are. This means that their price fluctuates during the trading day due to

the organic market.

Broadening:
ETFs provide diversification by investing in a variety of assets such as stocks, bonds, commodities, or a combination of these. ETFs, like common assets, provide access to a wide range of resources while lowering the risk associated with placing resources into specific protections.

Adaptability:
ETFs provide flexibility to investors by allowing them to trade at market prices throughout the trading day. This enables financial backers to respond quickly to economic events or take advantage of intraday trading opportunities. ETFs additionally enable the use of advanced exchanging systems, for example, limit orders, stop-loss orders, and options trading.

Reduced Expenses:
ETFs, on average, have lower cost proportions as compared to common assets. This is because ETFs often aim to replicate the performance of a specific index, such as the S&P 500, rather than effectively managing methods. ETFs are an appealing option for cost-conscious investors due to their lower charges.

Charge Expertise:
ETFs are well-known for their low expense ratios. Because of their unique form, ETFs can limit potential opportunities and capital increases circulations. This is performed through the production and recovery of in-kind offers, which aids in the provision of available opportunities till a financial supporter

sells their ETF shares.

Selection of Speculation Options:

ETFs provide a wide range of speculating options, including broad market file reserves, region explicit assets, security reserves, warehouse assets, and worldwide assets. Investors can select ETFs based on their investment objectives, risk tolerance, and market outlook.

Shared assets and ETFs both provide financial backers with access to expertly crafted, diverse portfolios. The choice between the two is based on characteristics such as speculation methods, cost considerations, liquidity preferences, and exchanging adaptability. Before making a venture decision, investors should carefully consider the asset's objectives, execution history, expenses, and risks. Speaking with a financial advisor can also provide significant guidance in selecting the most appropriate investment vehicle for individual needs.

Items and Precious Metals

Items and expensive metals are unmistakable resources that have long been sought after. They provide exceptional speculation, open opportunities, and serve as enhancing components in a well-balanced portfolio. Here is a list of goods and precious metals to consider as investment options:

Wares:

Types and Definitions:

products are raw commodities or necessary rural products that can be traded under normalized product trade agreements. They are broadly classified into four major groups: energy (including oil and petroleum gas), metals (including copper and aluminum), agricultural products (including wheat and corn), and animals (including cows and hoards).

Expansion Barrier:

Items have long been considered expansion support. When an economy expands, the cost of goods often rises since they are essential inputs to many businesses. Investing in products can assist protect against the dwindling purchasing power of government-issued money, as their qualities frequently value during inflationary periods.

Elements of the organic market:

Organic market forces influence the prices of items. Changes in global economic situations, international events, atmospheric conditions, and mechanical advancements can all have an impact on the organic market aspects of products. Financial backers who check these factors may be able to differentiate possible venture open doors in products.

Portfolio Expansion:

Remembering items for a venture portfolio can provide rewards. Products have traditionally had little in common with traditional asset types such as equities and bonds. This suggests that their value developments may differ from those of other enterprises, contributing in the reduction of overall portfolio risk.

Access via Subordinates:

Because of capability and determined prerequisites, investing directly in genuine products can be stimulating for individual financial backers. In any case, financial backers can gain access to goods via subordinates such as prospect agreements or trade exchanged products (ETCs). These venture structures enable financial supporters to participate in product cost developments without actually claiming the primary resources.

Metals of high value:
Types and Definitions:
Valuable metals such as gold, silver, platinum, and palladium are valued for their one-of-a-kind cases and intriguing features. They have long been seen as major value storage and a means of conserving wealth.

Resources for a safe haven:
During times of monetary instability or market volatility, precious metals are frequently viewed as refuge resources. When financial supporters seek refuge from volatile business sectors, they may turn to precious metals as a considerable store of value. Metals with a long history of preserving their value can provide protection against currency fluctuations and foreign threats.

Significantly Valuable Store:
Valuable metals have been used as a kind of money and a store of great value from the beginning of time. They are regarded as significant resources with distinct value. Investors commonly turn to precious metals to diversify their portfolios and save money in the long run.

Current Interest:

Aside from their role as substantial value repositories, precious metals have a critical modern interest. They are used in a variety of industries, including electronics, automobiles, jewelry, and medical services. Changes in modern interest can impact the prices of important metals, providing incredible opportunities for speculation.

Portfolio Assistance:
Financial backers usually use precious metals to hedge against expansion and money risks. During periods of expansion, the value of valuable metals will generally rise, providing protection against the depreciation of purchasing power. Because their properties are not directly related to specific money, precious metals can also operate as a hedge against cash devaluation or instability.

Venture Opportunities:
Various methods should be available for converting resources into valuable metals. Financial backers can purchase physical bullion in the form of bars or coins. They can, nevertheless, obtain openness through trade traded funds (ETFs), which hold actual metals or track the presence of valuable metals charges. Prospectus agreements and options also allow financial backers to exchange valuable metals on item trades.

It's critical to remember that investing in products and precious metals carries inherent risks. Cost volatility, international variables, and changes in organic market dynamics can all have an impact on the value of these resources. Similarly, as with any speculation, thorough research, understanding of market factors, and careful consideration of risk and reward are essential. Speaking with a financial expert can provide essential experience and guidance in incorporating products and precious metals into a venture procedure..

5

Investigating Speculations

Investigating Speculations

Major Investigation:

Identifying the Value. The fundamental evaluation is a process used by financial backers to examine the inherent worth of a product, such as a stock or bond. Central examination hopes to determine whether a venture is inflated or underestimated by analyzing the hidden variables that drive an organization's presentation.

The following is an outline of the essential investigation and its important components:

Fiscal summaries, which include the accounting report, pay announcement, and income explanation, provide the foundation of critical investigation. These assertions provide a comprehensive view of an organization's monetary exposure, liquidity, benefit, and income age. Financial backers can gain knowledge about an organization's financial well-being and evaluate its genuine capacity for future growth by breaking down these declarations.

Income and income evaluation entails evaluating an organization's verifiable and predicted profit development and income age. Financial backers assess an organization's ability to provide practical benefits by looking at factors such as income development rates, overall revenues, and income per offer. Correlations with industry peers and verifiable implementation can help identify patterns and assess an organization's seriousness.

Valuation Measurements:

Valuation measurements are used to determine whether security is overstated or understated. The cost-to-income proportion (P/E proportion), cost-to-sales proportion (P/S proportion), cost-to-book proportion (P/B proportion), and profit yield are all common valuation metrics. These ratios provide insight into how the market values a company in relation to its income, sales, book value, or profit installments. Financial investors use these metrics to assess the appeal of an enterprise and a fantastic opportunity.

Industry and Market Research:

Understanding the business elements and larger economic problems is a critical component of any substantial study. Financial backers consider elements such as market size, competitive environment, administrative climate, and macroeconomic tendencies. An industry evaluation determines the development potential and risks associated with an organization's working environment. The market research provides information on overall economic situations, financial backer feelings, and potentially open doors or risks.

The Executives' Opinion:

The management team is critical to the success of any firm. The primary examination comprises evaluating the supervisory crew's experience, history, and critical thinking skills. Financial backers look at things like corporate management, key drives, and the organization's response to problems or lucrative opportunities. A well-equipped and investor-friendly management team is frequently regarded as a positive indicator of long-term success.

Subjective elements:

In addition to quantitative examination, crucial inquiry incorporates subjective elements. These include elements that may be difficult to quantify, such as an organization's image esteem, protected invention, upper hands, and corporate culture. Subjective investigation enquires into immaterial viewpoints that can influence an organization's future prospects and competitive position.

Financial and Market Perspective:

The primary investigation addresses the broader monetary and market perspective. Factors such as finance costs, expansion, foreign risks, and industry trends can all have an impact on business decisions. Examining what these external factors might signify for an organization's activities and financial performance is an important aspect of the first research.

Central evaluation provides financial backers with a comprehensive understanding of an organization's financial well-being, growth prospects, and natural worth. It supports financial investors in making informed venture decisions based on an organization's fundamentals rather than solely on ephemeral market patterns. However, it is critical to remember that central examination has limitations and should be supported with other forms of inquiry and risk management measures.

While applying for the primary examination, investors should consider their venture goals, risk tolerance, and time frame. Speaking with a financial advisor or directing attentive research can also boost the viability of vital examination in uncovering speculation, openings, and risk administration.

Examining the Market in Depth. Specialized inspection is a tactic used by dealers and financial backers to deconstruct securities by focusing on verified price and volume data. It entails the use of outlines and other specialized markers to recognize examples, patterns, and possible exchange opportunities. The following is an outline of the specialized investigation and its essential components:

Value Diagrams:

Cost diagrams serve as the foundation for specialist analyses. They demonstrate the provable value developments of security throughout time. Line graphs, bar graphs, and candle graphs are all common types of price graphs. These diagrams provide visual representations of value examples and patterns, allowing professionals to identify support and opposition levels, trend lines, and graph designs.

Pattern Examination:

A pattern examination is a key concept in a specialized inquiry. It entails determining the long-term trend of a security's cost development. Vertical patterns are bullish, descending patterns are negative, and sideways patterns are range-bound. Experts employ trend lines, changing midpoints, and pattern pointers to determine the strength and length of a pattern. Understanding the dominating pattern helps merchants make informed decisions about joining or exiting positions.

Backing and Obstruction Levels:

On a graph, backing and obstruction levels are critical cost levels that act as roadblocks to cost development. Support levels are areas where purchasing interest is expected to be strong enough to prevent further cost drops. Conversely, opposition levels are areas where selling pressure is supposed to prevent additional cost increases. Recognizing these levels helps brokers make trading decisions because expenses frequently respond as they approach or pass through these levels.

Diagram Designs: Diagram designs are clear developments that appear on cost outlines and provide insights into probable future cost developments. Head and shoulders, two-sided tops and bottoms, triangles, and banners are common diagram designs. These examples show potential pattern inversions or continuation designs, which can help merchants forecast future cost activities.

Technical indicators are mathematical calculations that are applied to price and volume data to provide further insights into market patterns and momentum. Moving averages, the relative strength index (RSI), the moving average convergence divergence (MACD), and stochastic oscillators are examples of technical indicators. These indicators aid traders in identifying overbought or oversold levels, as well as confirming trends and generating trading signals.

Volume analysis is the study of the trading volume related with price fluctuations. Volume can reveal information about the strength of a trend as well as the chance of a trend reversal. High volume during price increases shows significant purchasing demand, whereas high volume during price drops indicates strong selling pressure. On-balance volume (OBV) and volume-weighted average price (VWAP) are two volume indicators that can be used to assess price changes and predict prospective market trends.

periods and Trading Strategies:
   Technical analysis can be used on a variety of periods, from intraday to long-term. Depending on their preferred trading timeline and goals, traders may employ a variety of technical tools and tactics. Some traders focus on short-term market changes and use tactics such as scalping or day trading, whereas others use a longer-term approach such as swing trading or position trading.

Technical analysis has limits and is dependent on historical price data, which may not always precisely anticipate future price movements. When making investment decisions, traders and investors should utilize technical analysis as one tool among many and consider other elements such as fundamental analysis, market sentiment, and risk management approaches.

Technical analysts frequently participate in continual learning and experimentation to improve their skills. Understanding market psychology, staying up to current on market news and happenings, and evaluating and updating trading methods on a regular basis are all critical components of good technical analysis. Consulting with experienced traders, attending educational seminars, and using respected technical analysis software can all help to improve the use of technical analysis in market charting.

Evaluating Financial Statements of a Corporation

Evaluating a company's financial accounts is critical for reviewing its financial health and performance. Financial statements provide a detailed picture of a company's financial situation, profitability, and cash flow.

Overview of how to examine firm financial accounts effectively:

Balance Sheet Analysis:

The balance sheet shows a company's financial situation at various moments in time. Consider the
Variables when examining the financial statement:

Assets:

Consider the composition and liquidity of the company's assets, which include cash, accounts receivable, inventory, and property, plant, and equipment (PPE).

Liabilities:

Examine the company's short- and long-term liabilities, such as accounts payable, loans, and long-term debt. Examine the debts' maturity dates and interest rates.

Equity of Shareholders: Examine the equity component of the corporation, which comprises common stock, retained earnings, and additional paid-in capital. Keep an eye out for any changes in equity over time.

Income Statement Analysis:

The income statement, also known as the profit and loss statement, summarizes a company's revenues, expenses, and profitability for a given time period. The following are important factors to consider while examining the income statement:

Revenue:

Examine the revenue sources and trends for the company. Examine the revenue growth rate and the revenue breakdown by product or service.

Expenses:

Examine the cost of goods sold, operating expenses, and other charges for the company. Keep an eye out for any noteworthy changes in expense levels or cost-cutting initiatives.

Profitability Ratios:

Calculate and analyze profitability ratios such as gross profit margin, operating margin, and net profit margin. To evaluate the company's profitability, compare these ratios to industry peers and previous performance.

Cash Flow Statement Analysis:

A cash flow statement provides information about a company's cash inflows and outflows over a certain time period.

Its three sections are operating activities, investment activities, and financing activities.

The following are important factors to consider while examining the cash flow statement:

Operating Cash Flow:
   Assess the firm's ability to earn cash from its primary operations. Compare changes in operating cash flow to changes in net income over time. Positive operating cash flow is often a good sign.

Investing Cash Flow:
   Examine the company's capital expenditures, acquisitions, and divestitures. Determine whether the corporation is investing in assets with long-term worth.

Examine the company's financing actions, such as issuing or repurchasing shares, incurring or repaying debt, or paying dividends. Examine the influence of financing decisions on the overall financial health of the organization.

Financial Ratios and Metrics:
   Financial ratios provide a quantitative assessment of a company's financial performance and aid in the comparison of that performance to industry peers or historical benchmarks.

The following are examples of common financial ratios:

Liquidity Ratios: Determine a company's ability to meet its

immediate obligations. The current ratio and the rapid ratio are two examples.

Using solvency ratios, you may assess a company's long-term financial stability and capacity to repay its loans. The interest coverage ratio and debt-to-equity ratio are two examples.

The phrase effectiveness Ratios:
Examine a company's ability to manage resources and generate income. The amount of changed inventory and updated accounts receivable are two examples.

Profitability Ratios:
Determine if a company can create profits in relation to its cash, assets, or equity.

Return on equity (ROE) and return on assets (ROA) are two examples.

Comparison and Trend Analysis:
Compare a company's financial statements over multiple periods to acquire a better understanding of its financial performance. Examine sales, profitability, and financial ratio trends. Comparisons with peers and competitors in the industry might provide further information about the company's relative performance and competitive position.

Consider qualitative elements that may have an impact on a company's financial performance in addition to quantitative factors. This includes evaluating industry dynamics, the competitive landscape, the regulatory environment, and company-specific aspects including management quality, brand reputation, and innovation capabilities. These qualitative considerations can have an impact on the understanding of financial statement data.

It is critical to understand that financial statement analysis is not a stand-alone assessment. Other types of analysis, such as industry analysis, market research, and macroeconomic considerations, should supplement it. Consider the limitations of financial statements, such as potential accounting biases or non-financial elements that may have an impact on a company's worth.

.

6

Building a Diversified Portfolio

Influence of Asset Allocation

Asset allocation is a basic investment technique that entails diversifying a portfolio among several asset classes such as stocks, bonds, cash, and alternative assets. The ability of asset allocation to balance risk and return, maximize performance, and provide stability amid market swings is what gives it its power. This article discusses the key benefits and principles of asset allocation, as well as practical recommendations for putting an effective allocation strategy into action.

Diversification:

Spreading Risk and Increasing Returns

Asset allocation enables investors to diversify their holdings across asset classes, thereby lowering the impact of individual investment risks. Investors might possibly boost returns while reducing total portfolio volatility by spreading investments among a number of assets such as stocks, bonds, and cash. Diversification serves as a risk management measure by ensuring that losses in one asset class are offset by gains in another.

Risk and Return Management

The value of asset allocation rests in determining the optimal risk-return balance depending on an investor's goals, time horizon, and risk tolerance. A well-diversified portfolio can assist in achieving this balance by allocating assets in a way that is consistent with the investor's goals. A younger investor with a longer time horizon, for example, may allocate a higher percentage to equities, which have traditionally provided higher returns but are also associated with higher volatility.

Market Volatility Management

The capacity of asset allocation to manage market volatility is one of its primary benefits. Different types of assets tend to respond differently in different market conditions. Stocks, for example, may outperform bonds during periods of economic development, whilst bonds may provide stability during moments of economic slump. Investors can decrease the impact of market swings on their total portfolio and potentially offset losses during stormy periods by diversifying across asset classes.

Rebalancing for Maximum Execution

To maintain the appropriate resource blend, the resource part requires periodic rebalancing. After some time, certain resource classes may outperform others, resulting in portfolio inequity.

Selling ventures that have appreciated and transferring assets that fail to meet projected resources for reestablishing the first objective designation are examples of rebalancing. This taught process assists financial backers in purchasing low and selling high, ensuring they stay focused on their long-term enterprise objectives.

Adapting Resource Portion to Individual Needs

Resource distribution is not a one-size-fits-all approach. It should be tailored to a person's financial goals, risk tolerance, and time horizon. Younger investors with a longer time horizon and better risk tolerance may prefer a more aggressive distribution, whereas older investors nearing retirement may prefer a more conservative practice. Working with a financial counselor can aid financial backers in determining the best resource percentage based on their specific circumstances.

The Role of Distribution Resource Classes

Choosing the best mix of resource types is part of resource distribution. Every resource class has unique characteristics and potential returns. Stocks provide growth potential but are more volatile, whilst bonds provide revenue and security but provide lesser returns. Money and elective speculations, such as land or products, provide additional widening. Understanding the characteristics of distinct resource classes is critical for developing a balanced portfolio.

The power of resource allocation resides in its ability to improve returns while managing risk. By diversifying their bets across several asset classes, investors can mitigate the impact of market fluctuations and achieve a higher risk-adjusted return. Standard rebalancing and tailoring the share to individual needs are critical components of a successful resource allocation system. Financial supporters can improve their portfolios, increase returns, and work toward long-term monetary goals by utilizing the power of resource allocation.

Building a Reasonable Portfolio Procedures

Building a decent portfolio is a critical step toward achieving long-term financial goals and managing venture risk.

Processes to consider while creating a significantly enhanced and adjusted portfolio:

Characterize Your Speculation aims:

Before constructing a portfolio, define your venture aims and time. Is it safe to state that you are saving for retirement, college, or a specific financial goal? Understanding your goals can help you choose the best resource allocation.

Assess Your Gamble Resilience:

Assessing your gamble resistance is critical since it affects the distribution of resources in your portfolio. A stronger risk resistance may lead to a more prominent allocation to development-focused resources such as equities, whilst a lower risk resilience may lead to a more prominent allocation to additional moderate resources such as securities.

Enhancement: .

Broadening is crucial for reducing risk and increasing rewards. Distribute your hypotheses over several resource classes, locations, and topographical districts. This broadening helps to mitigate the effect of unpredictability in any one region and may increase returns over time.

Designation of Resource Classes:

Determine the best mix of resource classes based on your risk profile and venture objectives. Stocks, on the other hand, offer larger long-term gains but are more volatile. Bonds, on the other hand, provide stability and pay. Consider including diverse resources such as land, products, or alternative guesses because their risk returns qualities.

Rebalancing:

Survey and rebalance your portfolio on a regular basis to maintain the optimal resource allocation. Market fluctuations can cause the weightings of various resources to deviate from your core goals. Rebalancing entails selling under performing resources and purchasing under performing resources in order to align the portfolio with your intended distribution.

Consider temporal Skyline:

Change your resource allocation based on your venture's temporal skyline. Longer-term goals may necessitate a more forceful distribution of values, but shorter-term goals may necessitate a more secure technique with a greater emphasis on fixed-pay protections.

Stay Informed:

Stay up to date on market trends, economic conditions, and developments in the venture scene. Audit and evaluate your portfolio's exhibition on a regular basis to ensure it is in accordance with your business objectives.

Seek Proficient Advice:

If you are unsure about constructing a suitable portfolio or are short on time or skill, consider seeing a financial advisor. They can help you evaluate your objectives and risk tolerance, as well as support you in constructing a portfolio that meets your needs.

Remember that building a good portfolio is a never-ending process. Regular review, appraisal, and revisions are required to ensure that your portfolio remains aligned with your financial objectives and adapts to changing economic conditions.

Examining Chance Resilience

Evaluating your risk tolerance is an important step in determining the best venture procedure and resource allocate

Key points to consider while assessing your gambling resilience:

Grasping Gamble:

Chance in successful financial planning refers to the possi-

61

bility of losing some or all of your speculation. It is vital to understand that all projects involve some level of risk. Understanding the many types of threats, for example, market risk, expansion risk, and liquidity risk, can enable you to make more educated decisions regarding the level of risk you will accept.

Speculation aims:

Explain your venture's aims and timetable. Is it possible to say that you are financially planning for short-term or long-term goals? Momentary goals may necessitate a more secure approach to protecting your head, whilst long-term goals may necessitate a greater ability to bear a chance to achieve better yields.

Risk Resistance Surveys:

A variety of financial foundations and venture stages conduct risk resilience surveys or appraisals. These polls often gather information about your financial situation, venture information, investment ambitions, and desire to tackle obstacles. The results might help you determine your level of risk tolerance and guide you in making investment decisions.

Profound Solace:

Consider how comfortable you are with the ups and downs of the venture markets. During times of market volatility, some financial backers may feel uneasy, while others may be stronger. Understanding your near-home solace with dangers can help you choose a suitable resource portion that corresponds to your mental capacity to endure fluctuations in venture values.

Monetary Capacity:

Determine your financial capacity to bear risk. Consider your current financial situation, pay dependability, and the availability of crisis reserves. Having a solid financial foundation can give a greater capacity to withstand risk and possibly recover from speculating losses.

Venture Information and Experience:

Consider your level of knowledge and experience. If you are new to smart money management or have limited information, you may initially have a lower risk tolerance. As your knowledge and expertise grow, you may become more receptive to taking on greater amounts of risk.

Expansion:

Enhancement plays an important role in risk management. A well-balanced portfolio that comprises a variety of asset classes will help to mitigate the impact of any particular speculation's performance on your overall portfolio. You can mitigate risks by spreading your speculations among several places and districts.

Regular Survey and Reassessment:

It is critical to audit and reassess your gambling resistance on a regular basis. Your gamble resistance may fluctuate over time due to a variety of circumstances such as changes in monetary conditions, individual aspirations, or economic situations. Rethinking your gamble resistance on a regular basis ensures that your speculating system remains in sync with your comfort level and aims.

Keep in mind that risk tolerance is an individual assessment that varies from person to person. It is critical to be honest with yourself about your level of comfort with risk and to discover a venture approach that aligns with your specific circumstances and financial ambitions. If necessary, consult with a financial advisor who can provide advice tailored to your specific situation.

Portfolio Management and Rebalancing

Overseeing and rebalancing your portfolio is critical to ensuring that it remains aligned with your speculating objectives and resistance to change.

Factors to consider when monitoring and rebalancing your portfolio:

Normal Checking:

Screen your portfolio's presentation on a regular basis. Keep an eye out for unique endeavors as well as standard resource allocation. This will aid you in identifying any significant variations from your desired designation and allowing you to make an appropriate move.

Set Rebalancing boundaries:

Establish specific boundaries that trigger the need for portfolio rebalancing. For example, you may decide to rebalance if the allocation to a given resource class deviates from your objective portion by a certain percentage (e.g., 5%). Setting defined boundaries promotes discipline and consistency in managing your portfolio.

Examining Resource Class Execution:

Evaluate the display of each resource class in your portfolio. Some resource classes may outflank others over time, causing changes in their relative loads. You can identify resource classes that have grown overweight or underweight by assessing the exhibition and making an appropriate move.

Redistribute and Purchase/Sell:

If your resource allocation has deviated significantly from your goal, redistributing your investments may be critical. This comprises selling some of the over represented resource class and buying more of the underrepresented resource class to return the portfolio to its target distribution. Rebalancing should be available by customary obligations, monetary inflows, or explicit venture sales and purchases.

Charge Suggestions:

Think about the obligation implications of rebalancing. Selling speculations with a high value may result in capital addition costs. Examine the impact of fees on your rebalancing options, and get advice from a cost expert if necessary.

Rebalancing Recurrence:

Determine how often you will rebalance your portfolio. Some financial backers prefer to rebalance on a regular basis, such as quarterly or yearly, whilst others prefer to rebalance when specific boundaries are reached. The appropriate recurrence is determined by your unique circumstances, economic circumstances, and the degree of float from your target portion.

Consider Exchange Expenses:

When rebalancing, keep exchange charges in mind. Trading guesses may result in business charges or other currency costs. Limit these costs by consolidating exchanges and selecting low-cost speculation options where possible.

Rethink Speculation Method:

During the rebalancing process, make a move to rethink your venture method. Examine your investment objectives, risk tolerance, and overall economic status. If necessary, make changes to your long-term speculating system to ensure it remains relevant and in accordance with your objectives.

Seek Skilled Direction:

Overseeing and rebalancing a portfolio can be difficult, especially as your speculative portfolio grows. Consider seeking professional guidance from a financial advisor who can provide tailored advice based on your unique circumstances and goals.

Remember that the portfolio board is a continuous cycle. Survey, screen, and rebalance your portfolio on a regular basis to maintain optimal resource distribution and adapt to changes in your venture goals and economic realities. By remaining proactive and controlled in managing your portfolio, you increase your chances of meeting your long-term financial goals.

7

Investing Resources in a Global Economy

Global Market Overview

A global market overview depicts the current state of various monetary business areas around the world. It contains the presentation, patterns, and factors that have a global impact on significant economies, stock exchanges, security markets, monetary standards, and products. Here are a few key points to consider while providing a global market overview:

Global Financial Situation:

Begin by assessing the global economic situation. Discuss significant monetary indicators, such as GDP growth rates, expansion, unemployment, and national bank strategies. Highlight significant regions or countries that are driving global economic growth or facing challenges.

Exchanges of securities:

Give an overview of major financial transactions from around the world. Examine significant indices such as the S&P

500 (US), FTSE 100 (UK), Nikkei 225 (Japan), DAX (Germany), and Shanghai Composite (China). Include ongoing execution, patterns, and aspects influencing these business sectors, such as corporation income, international events, and financial backer sentiment.

Markets for Security:

Discuss the state of the global security markets, including government and corporate securities. Examine significant security yields, such as the US Depository yield curve or the German Bond yield. Consider factors influencing security market developments, such as financial arrangement decisions, expansion expectations, and monetary indicators.

Monetary criteria:

Give an overview of major cash matches and their new exhibition. Discuss issues influencing cash markets, such as loan cost differentials, international events, and national bank arrangements. Include any notable financial patterns or developments, such as variations in return rates or cash mediation.

Items:

Examine the exhibition of important wares such as oil, gold, silver, copper, and rural products. Discuss the factors that influence ware markets, such as organic market aspects, international tensions, and meteorological conditions. Include any significant cost developments or emerging tendencies in the item area.

International Events:

Discuss international events that may have an impact on global business sectors. This could include exchange tensions, political campaigns, strategic shifts, or disputes in diverse areas. Determine how these events may affect financial backer sentiment, market volatility, and monetary outlook.

Business Sectors in Development:

Display the exposition and trends in expanding business sectors such as China, India, Brazil, and Southeast Asian countries. Examine their financial development opportunities, strategic advancements, and lucrative enterprise opportunities. Highlight any new risks or opportunities associated with investing in expanding company areas.

Global National Bank Activities:

Discuss the financial strategies and activities of major national banks, including the United States. Central Bank, European National Bank, Bank of Japan, and People's Bank of China. Examine loan cost options, quantitative enabling programs, and other strategy estimations that may have a significant impact on global business sectors.

Market Risks and Position:

Summarize the major threats and weaknesses confronting global company sectors, such as exchange pressures, international conflicts, expansion issues, or the impact of new developments. Give your perspective on the global business sectors, taking into mind both potential opportunities and potential challenges.

It is critical to remember that a global market overview should be updated on a regular basis to reflect the most recent economic conditions and trends. Factors influencing global business sectors can shift quickly, therefore it's critical to keep informed and constantly monitor global monetary and market developments.

Global Stocks and Bonds

Global stocks and securities play a significant role in diversifying investment portfolios and providing access to global economic sectors. Here are a few key points to consider while analyzing global stocks and bonds:

Global Stocks:
a. Global Market Opportunities: Investing in global stocks allows investors to access several opportunities outside of their own market. It allows organizations functioning in many areas, districts, and economies to be more open.

b. Advantages of Expansion:
Including international stocks in a portfolio might help to reduce fixation risk. Various countries and regions may have varying monetary cycles, political contexts, and economic conditions, which can aid in balancing bets on a single market.

c. Area and Industry Openness:
Global business sectors frequently provide access to extraordinary areas and companies that may not be well-served by domestic business sectors. For example, expanding company sectors may provide opportunities in innovation, consumer goods, or regular assets.

d. Money Openness:

Investing in global stocks demonstrates cash openness. Changes in return rates can have an impact on worldwide speculating earnings. This provides an additional degree of risk and likely reward for financial backers.

Bonds around the world:

a. Broadening and Risk Management: Global bonds can supplement a fixed-income portfolio beyond domestic bonds. They provide access to varied lending rates, credit risks, and expansion factors across global economies, assisting with risk management.

b. Yield and Pay Opportunities:

When compared to domestic securities, international securities can offer more tempting yield and pay opportunities, particularly in areas where loan rates are higher or credit spreads are wider.

c. Cash Risk and Supporting:

Because pay and head reimbursements are sometimes stated in new monetary forms, global bonds can entail money risk. Financial supporters must consider the impact of currency fluctuations on their profits. When necessary, supporting strategies might be used to mitigate monetary risk.

d. Sovereign and Corporate Securities:

Global security markets include both sovereign and corporate securities issued by government-run agencies. Each provides distinct risk and return profiles, and investors can choose based on their risk tolerance and investment objectives.

Considerations for Investing in Global Stocks and Bonds:

a. Research and a suitable amount of effort:

Before pursuing speculation options, lead a detailed evaluation of global company sectors, economies, and specific companies or backers. Understand the target country's political, economic, and administrative landscape.

b. Nation and Cash Risks:

Different countries may present interesting risks, such as political unrest, administrative changes, or financial unpredictability. Evaluate these risks and their potential impact on initiatives.

c. Investing in Global Business Sectors:

Investors can invest in global stocks and securities through a variety of vehicles, including as common stocks, exchange-traded funds (ETFs), or individual protections.

When selecting a venture vehicle, consider costs, liquidity, and additional benefits.

Effective Direction:

Looking for guidance from a monetary counselor or speculation expert versed in global money management can be beneficial for financial supporters who are new to international business sectors or lose out on the opportunity to lead broad exploration.

Investing in international equities and bonds necessitates careful consideration of various factors, such as country-specific risks, currency openness, and the potential benefits of expansion. Financial backers can take advantage of global opportunities and potentially boost risk-adjusted returns by incorporating global interests into a broader portfolio.

Trade Rates and Money Risks

Trade rates and money bets play an important role in global exchange, ventures, and global monetary business sectors. Here are a few key issues to consider when analyzing trade rates and cash bets:

Rates of Exchange:
a. Definition:

Trade rates deal with the value of one currency in comparison to another. They determine the exchange rate for monetary forms. Trade rates fluctuate due to a variety of factors such as organic market aspects, loan fee differentials, financial indicators, international events, and market sentiment.

b. Trade Rate Varieties:

Spot rates (current trade prices for assured exchanges), forward rates (trade rates agreed upon for future exchanges), and ostensible vs true trade rates (taking into account expansion differentials) are all types of trade rates.

c. Trade Rates Can Be Drifting or stable:

Trade rates can be either drifting or stable. Cash values in drifting conversion standard frameworks change totally based on market effects. National banks mediate in fixed conversion scale frameworks to maintain explicit conversion scale levels

74

by trading monetary standards.

d. Exchange Influence:

Trade rates have a direct impact on global exchange rates. Cash appreciation (reinforcement) can make a country's commodities more expensive and imports less expensive, potentially altering exchange rates. Money depreciation (debilitation) can have the opposite effect, making sends out more serious.

Money Peril:

a. Exchange risk arises from changes in return rates between the time an exchange is agreed upon and the time it is settled. It can have an impact on the productivity of global exchanges, particularly for organizations involved in import/send-out operations.

b. Risk of Misinterpretation:

The risk of interpretation has an impact on global organizations with auxiliaries working in various monetary standards. Variations in return rates can affect the value of unfamiliar auxiliaries' resources, liabilities, incomes, and benefits when converted into detailing cash for the parent organization.

c. Financial Risk:

Monetary gamble, also known as working or cutthroat gamble, refers to the potential impact of conversion scale developments on the overall seriousness and benefit of an organization. It can have an impact on an organization's cost structure, evaluating techniques, and market position.

d. Supporting Money Risks: Various assisting techniques can

be used to alleviate money risks. These include using forward agreements, cash fates, options, or money trades to secure in-return rates for future transactions. However, supporting safeguards against unfavorable financial developments can also limit expected gains.

Factors Influencing Trade Rates and Money Risks:

a. Fees for loans:

Financing cost differentials between countries can have an impact on trade rates. Higher financing costs, for the most part, attract new speculation, expanding and possibly reinforcing interest in money.

b. Money Suggestions:

Financial factors such as GDP growth, expansion rates, business information, exchange adjustments, and monetary arrangements can all have an impact on trade rates. Solid financial performance frequently leads to cash appreciation, whereas poor financial performance can lead to devaluation.

c. Political and international variables:

Political security, government strategies, international events, and trade relations between countries can all have an impact on trade rates and acquaint volatility with money markets.

d. Market Sentiment:

Market participants' perceptions, assumptions, and opinions about a country's monetary prospects can drive swapping scale developments. Money market volatility can be caused by hypotheses and financial backer emotions.

Monitoring Money Risks:

a. Openness Survey:

Assess your openness to money takes a chance by distinguishing exchanges, speculations, or business tasks that include various monetary standards.

b. Risk Management Methodologies:

Consider implementing risk in the executive's systems to mitigate cash risks, such as using supporting instruments or differentiating money openings.

c. Examining and Investigating:

Keep up to date on global financial and political developments that may have an impact on trade rates. Screen cash markets and lead the thorough investigation to make informed decisions.

d. Counsel who is knowledgeable:

For complex money risk the board needs or on the other hand, enormous openings, look for direction from monetary consultants, money subject matter experts, or chance administration experts.

Trade rates and money gambles are significant contemplation for organizations participating in global exchange and financial backers with openness to unfamiliar business sectors. Understanding the elements of trade rates, overseeing money chances, and executing proper gamble-the-board systems can assist with

MONEY SEED OF HAPPINESS

alleviating likely antagonistic impacts and upgrading monetary navigation.

Putting resources into Developing Business sectors

Putting resources into developing business sectors can offer interesting open doors and potential for appealing returns, yet it additionally accompanies particular dangers and contemplation. Here are a few central issues to consider while examining putting resources into developing business sectors:

Meaning of Developing Business Sectors:

a. Developing business sectors allude to nations that are encountering fast financial development and going through critical industrialization and advancement. These business sectors ordinarily have lower per capita pay, less-created framework, and advancing monetary frameworks contrasted with created markets.

b. Developing business sectors can be tracked down across various districts, including Asia, Latin America, Eastern Europe, Africa, and the Center East. Instances of developing business sector nations incorporate China, India, Brazil, South Africa, Mexico, and numerous others.

Expected Advantages of Putting Resources into Developing Business Sectors:

a. Higher Development Potential:
   Developing business sectors frequently offer higher financial

development rates contrasted with created markets. Fast pop-ulace development, urbanization, extending working classes, and rising buyer spending add to this development potential.

b. Broadening:

Putting resources into developing business sectors gives expansion benefits by adding openness to economies that may not be profoundly connected with created markets. This can assist with lessening general portfolio risk and possibly improve returns.

c. Underestimated Resources:

My Developing business sectors might offer venture open doors in areas and organizations that are underestimated or ignored by standard financial backers. These business sectors can introduce alluring valuations compared with their develop-ment potential.

d. Admittance to Normal Assets:

Many developing business sectors are plentiful in regular assets like oil, gas, minerals, and rural items. Putting resources into these economic sectors can give openness to the worldwide interest in these assets

Dangers and Difficulties of Putting Resources into Developing Business Sectors:

a. Political and Administrative Dangers:

Developing corporate sectors can meet political flimsiness, government involvement, defilement, and administrative weaknesses. Changes in government arrangements can alter venture conditions and production.

b. Financial Unpredictability:

Developing business sectors can confront more notable monetary instability contrasted with additional grownup economies. Factors like expansion, money variations, financial unbalanced qualities, and outer shocks can urge expanded market unpredictability.

c. Cash Hazard:

Putting resources into developing company sectors involves openness to money risk. Vacillations in return rates can damage the value of speculations when changed over once more into the financial backer's home cash.

d. Liquidity and Market Proficiency:

A few emerging business sectors can have lower liquidity and less competent business sectors compared with created markets. This can provoke challenges in executing exchanges and esteeming ventures accurately.

e. Legitimate and Administration Issues:

Overall sets of regulations and corporate administration standards in emerging business sectors could vary from those in created marketplaces, possibly impacting financial backer certainties and the dependability of monetary facts.

Venture Approaches and Methodologies:

a. Research and A decent degree of effort:

Careful research and investigation of specific nations, territories, and organizations are crucial. Survey aspects, for example, financial markets, political strength, administrative climate, strategic approaches, and corporate administration standards.

b. Expansion:

Spread endeavors across different emerging business sectors, places, and resource classes to reduce focus danger. Enhancement aids catch the anticipated prospective benefit of diverse business sectors while lowering the effect of particular country-explicit risks.

c. Long haul Viewpoint:

Putting resources into developing business areas typically involves a drawn-out speculating skyline. Financial and market cycles in these business sectors might be more characterized, and perseverance might be expected to comprehend the maximal capacity of speculations.

d. Dynamic Administration:

Consider dynamic administration procedures to examine the extraordinary risks and lucrative open doors in rising business sectors. Gifted shop chiefs or venture gurus can properly screen and adjust portfolios because of growing economic problems.

Contemplation for Individual Financial Backers:

a. Risk Resilience:

Evaluate your risk resistance and grasp that putting resources into emerging business sectors delivers more significant degrees of danger contrasted with putting resources into created markets.

b. Effective Direction:

Assuming that you're new to putting resources into emerging business sectors or miss the mark on crucial ability, consider looking for instruction from monetary counselors or speculation professionals with knowledge in these business sectors.

c. Observing and Survey:

Routinely analyze your endeavors and remain informed about developments in expanding business sectors. Remain refreshed on monetary markers, political occasions, and administrative alterations that can influence your speculations.

Putting investment into growing business sectors might offer the opportunity for compelling returns and portfolio widening. In any case, it's necessary to methodically examine the threats, lead an extensive examination, and explore a drawn-out venture approach. By figuring out the exceptional aspects of expanding business sectors and accepting suitable venture procedures, financial backers can place themselves to make the most of the learning experiences these business sectors provide.

8

Retirement Contribution

Fundamentals of Retirement Planning

Retirement planning is an important element of personal budgeting since it includes setting goals and doing everything it
takes to ensure financial security in retirement. Here are a few
key points to consider when researching retirement planning
fundamentals:

Determine Your Retirement Goals:

a. Begin by envisioning your ideal retirement lifestyle. Consider
aspects such as desired exercises, itinerary items, medical care
requirements, and specific goals you have for your retirement
years.

b. Determine your estimated retirement age and the number of
years you plan to spend in retirement. This can help you assess
the scope of your retirement investing money requirements.

Examine the Current Economic Situation:

a. Examine your current financial situation, including pay, expenses, reserve cash, and business initiatives. Examine your assets, liabilities, and income to get a sense of your overall financial situation.

b. Consider any existing retirement accounts, such as employer-sponsored plans (e.g., 401(k)) or individual retirement accounts (IRAs). Keep an eye on the equilibrium and commitment rates.

Calculate Retirement Costs:

a. Calculate your typical retirement expenses, such as housing, medical services, daily living expenses, travel, and recreational activities. Consider growth and potential lifestyle changes.

b. Recognize any typical sources of income throughout retirement, such as government-backed retirement benefits, annuity plans, or rental income. Determine the gap between your estimated costs and pay sources.

Create a Retirement Savings Plan:

a. Set a retirement reserve money goal based on your estimated expenses and desired style of life. Consider consulting with a financial advisor to determine an appropriate reserve funds aim.

b. Create a financial strategy to allocate assets to retirement reserve accounts. Plan to contribute to retirement accounts on a regular basis, taking advantage of any business matching programs or tax breaks.

c. In light of your risk tolerance and time horizon, consider diversifying your retirement reserve funds among multiple venture vehicles, such as equities, securities, common assets, or trade traded reserves (ETFs).

Increase Retirement Records and Benefits:

a. Add to your burden advantaged retirement records, such as 401(k), 403(b), or IRAs, to increase your reserve funds potential and take advantage of any business matching obligations.

b. When you reach a certain age, research the rules and guidelines governing retirement funds, such as contribution restrictions, withdrawal penalties, and required minimum distributions (RMDs).

Monitor Venture Risk:

a. Examine and adjust your speculation portfolio on a regular basis based on your risk tolerance, time horizon, and financial objectives. Consider an improved speculation approach that balances risk and potential returns.

b. Consider the impact of expansion on your reserve funds. Ventures with growth potential can help you safeguard the purchasing power of your retirement benefits in the long run.

Consider Medical Care and Security:

a. Plan for medical expenses in retirement. Examine options for health care coverage, long-term care protection, or Federal medical insurance to ensure enough inclusion for clinical requirements.

b. Consider whether you need life insurance, disability insurance, or other types of protection to protect yourself and your loved ones from unexpected events.

Survey and change your arrangement on a regular basis:

a. Return to your retirement plan on a regular basis to assess progress, make modifications in response to changing situations, and stay focused on your goals.

b. Consider seeking advice from a financial advisor with retirement experience who can assist you in navigating complex financial decisions and streamlining your retirement process.

Retirement planning takes careful consideration, consistent savings, and informed independent direction. You can make progress toward a financially secure and pleasant retirement by identifying clear objectives, reviewing what is happening, and implementing a balanced retirement plan.

Individual Retirement Accounts (IRAs) are a type of retirement account.

Individual Retirement Accounts (IRAs) are well-known retirement investment funds vehicles that provide charge benefits to individuals. Here are a few key points to consider when reviewing Individual Retirement Accounts (IRAs):

IRA Definition and Types:

a. A Singular Retirement Account (IRA) is a tax-advantaged retirement bank account available to citizens in the United States.

b. Traditional IRAs, Roth IRAs, SEP IRAs (Improved on Representative Benefits), and Straightforward IRAs (Investment funds Impetus Match Plan for Workers) are the several types of IRAs.

IRA Customary:

a. Commitments:
   Commitments to a Customary IRA are frequently tax deductible, which means you may be able to deduct the commitment amount from your available salary for the year.

b. Charge Handling:
   A Customary IRA's assets develop charge conceded, which means you don't pay charges on the profit until you withdraw the funds at retirement.

c. RMDs (Required Minimum Distributions): RMDs are the minimum amounts you must withdraw each year commencing at the age of 72 (about 2022). These withdrawals are primarily based on personal expenses.

The Roth IRA:

a. Commitments:

Commitments to a Roth IRA are made with after-charge dollars, which means you do not receive a quick duty deduction for your contributions.

b. Charge Handling:

The funds in a Roth IRA grow tax-free, and qualifying withdrawals during retirement are also tax-free.

c. There are no RMDs:

RMDs are not required for Roth IRAs during the record holder's lifetime. This makes them appealing to persons who do not need to pull out reserves straight once and must provide the record to recipients.

IRA SEP:

a. SEP IRAs are for self-employed individuals and entrepreneurs.

b. Commitments:

Commitments to a SEP IRA are tax deductible for the business, and the record proprietor does not pay taxes on the commitments until withdrawal.

c. Commitments of the Manager:

Businesses create obligations for eligible employees, and every qualified representative receives a similar level of commitment.

Simple IRA:

a. Basic IRAs are designed for independent businesses with less than 100 representatives.

b. Commitments:
Contributions to a Basic IRA are tax deductible for both corporations and representatives.

c. Managers must match a specific level of worker commitments or make a non-elective commitment to every qualifying representative.

Cutoff points for commitment and qualification:

a. The IRS establishes IRA contribution restrictions, which can alter each year. Starting about 2023, the annual contribution limit for Traditional and Roth IRAs will be $6,000, or $7,000 for persons aged 50 or older (get up to speed commitments).

b. Qualification to contribute to an IRA is based on criteria such as wage, job status, and cooperation in business-sponsored retirement programs.

Rollovers and Transformations of IRAs:

a. Rollover IRA:
People can transfer assets from one IRA to the next or from a certified boss-sponsored plan (e.g., 401(k)) to an IRA without incurring costs or penalties.

b. IRA Modification:
People can transfer assets from a traditional IRA to a Roth IRA,

which may trigger an available event because the transferred amount is recognized as available pay at the time of conversion.

Early Withdrawal Penalties:

a. Both traditional and Roth IRAs contain penalties for early withdrawals prior to the age of 5912, with specific exemptions. Early withdrawals from Traditional IRAs may also be subject to annual expense.

Contemplation:

a. Expansion:

IRAs provide an opportunity to supplement retirement investment funds beyond manager-managed plans.

b. Effective Direction:

Consult with a financial advisor or a duty expert to determine the best IRA type, commitment structure, and retirement reserve funds strategy for your specific financial circumstances and aspirations.

Individual Retirement Accounts (IRAs) provide people with a tax-advantaged way to save for retirement. Understanding the various types of IRAs, contribution limitations, fee ideas, and withdrawal requirements can help consumers make informed decisions about their retirement savings strategy. Working with a financial consultant or spending expert can provide tailored advice based on specific needs and goals.

Boss-Supported Retirement Plans (401(k), for example)

Boss-supported retirement plans, such as 401(k) plans, are well-known retirement investment funds vehicles provided by management to help employees save for the future. Here are a few key points to consider while researching employer-sponsored retirement plans:

Plan 401(k):

a. Definition:
A 401(k) plan is a tax-advantaged retirement investment fund plan that employers offer to their employees.

b. Commitments:
Representatives can contribute a portion of their pay to the 401(k) plan, most typically through financial derivations. These commitments are per-charged, which means that they are deducted from the representative's available pay.

c. Manager Matching Commitments: Many firms offer a matching commitment, in which they contribute a specified percentage of the representative's salary to the 401(k) plan based on a predetermined formula. Boss matching can essentially boost retirement savings.

d. Tax breaks:
Commitments to a traditional 401(k) plan develop charge conceded, which means the assets are not subject to charges until they are withdrawn after retirement. This takes into

account prospective duty investment funds in the long run.

e. Restrictions on Commitment:

The IRS establishes annual commitment restrictions for 401(k) plans. Starting approximately 2023, the maximum amount is $20,500, or $27,000 for persons aged 50 or older (get up to speed commitments).

f. Vesting:

The term vesting refers to the representative's accountability for obligations. Managers may impose a vesting plan, which requires employees to labor for a set period of time before becoming fully vested in boss commitments.

Other Employer-Funded Retirement Plans:

a. Characterized Benefit Plans: Characterized benefit plans, also known as benefits plans, provide workers with a certain monthly payment during retirement based on criteria such as compensation history and lengths of administration. The venture and life span gambles bear the business.

b. Plan 403(b):

403(b) plans are similar to 401(k) plans, but they are only available to representatives of select duty-free organizations, such as government-funded schools and not-for-profit organizations.

c. 457 Plans:

Government employees and certain non-legislative representatives, such as members of duty excluded associations, have access to 457 plans. They provide benefits similar to 401(k) plans.

d. The Frugality Reserve Funds Plan (TSP) is a retirement reserve funds plan for government representatives and individuals from officially attired administrations. It has features similar to 401(k) programs, such as charging conceded obligations and boss coordination.

Benefits of Employer-Supported Retirement Plans:

a. Commitments to employer-sponsored retirement plans are withdrawn directly from the worker's paycheck, making it easier to save consistently.

b. Manager Matching Commitments: Manager matches are essentially free money and can significantly improve retirement reserve funds.

c. Charge Benefits: Pre-charge money are used to make contributions to traditional 401(k) plans, reducing the representative's available salary. This takes into account prospective investment funds for expenses throughout the commitment years.

d. Potential Speculation Development: Retirement plans typically offer a variety of venture options, allowing employees to grow their investment capital over time.

.

e. Convenience:
Representatives can often stay up with their retirement funds

93

while changing jobs and have the option of transferring assets into a single retirement account (IRA) or another business' retirement plan.

Contemplation:

a. Venture Options: Examine the speculating options available under the business-supported retirement plan. Consider distinguishing projects based on risk tolerance and retirement goals.

b. Rates of Commitment:

Contribute enough to the retirement plan to take advantage of any company matching obligations, as it addresses a rapid profit from speculation.

c. Vesting Schedule:

Understand the company commitment vesting plan and its impact on your retirement investing funds if you quit the corporation.

Other Retirement Benefits and Government-Managed Retirement Plans

Government-managed retirement and other retirement benefits play a significant role in providing financial assistance during retirement. Here are a few key points to consider while researching government-sponsored retirement and other retirement benefits:

Government-sponsored retirement:

a. Definition:

Government-sponsored retirement is a governmental program in the United States that provides qualified individuals with retirement compensation, handicap benefits, and survivor benefits.

b. Qualification:

To be eligible for Government-managed retirement benefits, you must have accrued an adequate number of credits through work and payment of Government-backed retirement charges. The number of credits necessary depends on your introduction to the world year.

c. FRA (Full Retirement Age):

The FRA is the age at which you can begin receiving full Federal retirement aide benefits. It ranges from 66 to 67, depending on your introduction to the world year. Benefits can be guaranteed as early as age 62, but they will be reduced.

d. Benefits Calculation:

Government controlled retirement benefits are based on your average monthly profit and your FRA. The amount you receive can vary depending on the age you choose to receive benefits.

e. Changes in the cost of several everyday items (COLAs):

COLAs, or changes made to represent expansion, are what govern government-managed retirement benefits. COLAs anticipate keeping up with the purchasing power of advantages over the long term.

f. Spousal and Survivor Benefits: In light of their accomplice's profit record, companions may be eligible for Government controlled retirement benefits. If a companion dies, survivors may be eligible for survivor benefits.

Annuity Agreements:

a. Definition:
Benefits plans are retirement benefit plans that are supported by corporations in order to provide a consistent revenue stream to representatives during retirement.

b. Annuity Plan Types:
There are two types of benefit plans: defined benefit designs and defined commitment plans.

Advantage Plans with Characteristics:
These plans guarantee a specific benefit sum based on characteristics such as compensation history and lengths of administration. Bosses incur the risk of speculation and life-changing decisions.

Characterized Commitment Plans:
These plans, such as 401(k) plans, allow representatives to contribute a portion of their pay to a single retirement account. The potential benefit is dependent on pledges, venture execution, and individual choices.

c. Dissemination and vesting:
Benefits designs commonly include vesting systems that determine a worker's liability for commitments. Changes

in appropriation options include single-amount installments, annuity options, and rollovers to individual retirement accounts (IRAs).

Other Benefits of Retirement:

a. Individual Retirement Accounts (IRAs): IRAs are private retirement accounts that consumers can contribute to on a tax-advantaged basis. They provide flexibility in investment decisions and can supplement other retirement benefits.

b. Employee Stock Ownership Plans (ESOPs):
ESOPs are retirement plans that invest primarily in the company's shares. They provide employees with a stake in the company and can be a valuable retirement resource.

c. Health insurance:
Government medical care is a bureaucratic health-care coverage program for persons over the age of 65. It allows for the inclusion of specific clinical charges during retirement. Employers may also provide retirees with medical coverage, though this is less prevalent nowadays.

Making Plans for Retirement Benefits:

a. Qualification and Advantage Calculations:
Learn about the standards and estimates for Federal retirement assistance, annuities, and other retirement benefits. Consider consulting a financial advisor or using online mini-computers to estimate your future retirement salary.

b. Save and give back:

Make the most of your reserve money by contributing to manager-sponsored plans like as 401(k)s or IRAs to increase your retirement benefits.

c. Increase Retirement Pay:

Consider diversifying your retirement income sources to reduce your reliance on a single source. This can assist protect against potential changes in benefit initiatives or market fluctuations.

d. Change and Survey:

Audit your retirement accounts and benefit systems on a regular basis to ensure they are in sync with your changing circumstances, financial ambitions, and the changing landscape of retirement benefits.

It is critical to remember that retirement benefit projects and qualification regulations differ by country and can alter over time. Understanding the specific rules and regulations in your area, as well as seeking professional advice when necessary, will help you make informed decisions regarding your retirement planning.

Consider the following real estate investments:

By mid-career, you may have saved enough money to put towards real estate investments. Real estate can provide potential revenue streams through rental properties as well as the opportunity for long-term gain. To make informed selections in this asset class, conduct extensive study and due diligence.

Examine your insurance coverage:

As your obligations grow, be sure you have enough insurance to protect your assets, income, and loved ones. Consider policies such as life insurance, disability insurance, and liability insurance. Consult an insurance specialist to assess your needs and discover the best coverage for you.

Seek expert help if necessary:

Consider talking with a knowledgeable financial advisor if you are feeling overwhelmed or unclear about your investment decisions. They can offer specialized advice, objective insights, and assistance in navigating difficult financial concerns. Look for advisors that are knowledgeable about mid-career investments and have a fiduciary duty to operate in your best interests.

Align investment growth and liquidity:

While it is critical to seek investment growth, it is also critical to retain appropriate cash. Mortgages, college expenditures, and other obligations are common financial burdens in mid-career. Make sure you have adequate finances available to address short-term requirements and emergencies.

Regularly monitor and assess your investments:

Review your investment portfolio on a regular basis and make modifications as appropriate. Rebalance your portfolio on a regular basis to ensure correct asset allocation.

Keep up to date on market trends, economic conditions, and changes in tax legislation that may have an influence on your investing plan.

Remember that mid-career investments necessitate a deliberate approach that is in line with your changing financial goals, risk tolerance, and life circumstances. You may make informed decisions that promote your long-term financial success by being proactive, diversifying your investments, and getting professional guidance when necessary.

Nearing Retirement:
  Keeping and Increasing Your Wealth
  As you approach retirement age, it is vital to focus on protecting and expanding your wealth in order to ensure a comfortable and financially secure future. Consider the following ways to protect and improve your financial well-being as you approach this major milestone:

Determine your retirement objectives:

Set specific financial goals and define your retirement lifestyle. Consider your intended retirement age, your estimated expenses, your healthcare bills, and any legacy arrangements. Understanding your goals will help you make better investing selections and predict how much money you'll need in retirement.

Examine your portfolio of investments:
  Examine your financial portfolio and make changes to line it with your evolving needs. As retirement approaches, many people move to a more conservative investment strategy to protect their collected money. To maintain stability while potentially delivering consistent returns, balance growth-oriented

investments with income-producing assets and lower-risk options.

Diversify your investment portfolio:

Diversification is still important as you approach retirement. To lower risk and boost the potential for consistent returns, diversify your assets among asset classes, industries, and geographical locations. To develop a well-rounded portfolio, consider combining stocks, bonds, real estate, and other alternative investments.

Concentrate on money generation:

Prioritize investments that provide consistent income to enhance your retirement savings. Dividend-paying equities, bonds, annuities, and rental property are all potential income sources. You can maintain a consistent cash flow during retirement while maintaining your principal by focusing income-producing investments.

Control your risk exposure:

Protecting your wealth becomes increasingly critical as retirement approaches. Assess your risk tolerance and make appropriate adjustments to your investments. Reduce your exposure to extremely volatile investments and consider measures like hedging or utilizing stop-loss orders to reduce downside risk. Consult with a financial professional to identify the best risk management strategy for your scenario.

Consider the following tax-saving strategies:

To optimize your retirement savings, consider tax-efficient investment alternatives. Consider contributing to tax-advantaged retirement funds such as IRAs or 401(k)s. Consider tax-efficient investment vehicles such as index funds or tax-managed funds, which seek to reduce taxable payouts.

Review your retirement plan on a regular basis:

Review your retirement plan on a regular basis to ensure that it is still in line with your goals. Consider changes in your financial situation, market conditions, and developing retirement needs. To improve your retirement approach, adjust your plan as needed and seek professional advice.

Make a healthcare budget:

Healthcare costs can have a substantial influence on your retirement savings. Examine Medicare coverage as well as extra insurance choices. Consider purchasing long-term care insurance to protect yourself against the prospective costs of long-term care. Understanding and budgeting for healthcare bills in retirement will aid in the preservation of your wealth and financial security.

Seek expert assistance:

Because retirement planning can be complicated, working with a knowledgeable financial advisor can be beneficial. An advisor may evaluate your specific position, create a customized retirement plan, and provide continuous advice. Look for advisors that have experience with retirement planning and have a fiduciary duty to operate in your best interests.

Stay educated and adaptable:

Keep up with financial news, market trends, and regulatory developments that may affect your retirement planning. Maintain a flexible approach and be ready to adjust your investment strategy as needed. Staying educated will allow you to make more informed judgments and navigate any unexpected problems.

Approaching retirement necessitates a thorough and intentional approach to preserving and growing your wealth. You can position yourself for a financially secure and satisfying retirement by reassessing your investment portfolio, focusing on income creation, limiting risk, and getting professional assistance. Remember that keeping proactive and planning ahead of time are essential for reaching your retirement goals.

9

Investing in Your Golden Years

Investing in Your Golden Years

Determine your risk tolerance and then make prudent finan-cial decisions. It entails laying a financial foundation that will support your desired lifestyle while also providing long-term income during your retirement years.

Some things to think about when investing for your retirement years:

Determine your retirement requirements:

Begin by determining your retirement financial needs. Take into account your intended lifestyle, anticipated expenses, and any specific goals or plans you have for your elder years. This research will assist you in determining the amount of savings and income required to maintain your retirement lifestyle.

Calculate your retirement savings goal:

Once you've determined your retirement needs, determine

your target savings goal. Think about things like life expectancy, inflation, and possible healthcare bills. To set an acceptable retirement savings objective, you can use retirement calculators or talk with a financial counselor.

Start saving early and consistently:

When it comes to retirement savings, time is your most valuable asset. The earlier you begin saving, the more time your investments have to compound. Contribute consistently to your retirement accounts, such as 401(k)s, IRAs, or pension plans, and take advantage of any company matching contributions that are available to you.

Expand your speculating portfolio:

Expansion is critical for managing risk and increasing rewards in your retirement projects. Spread your investments over several asset classes, for example, equities, bonds, land, and possibly alternative speculations, depending on your risk tolerance and investment objectives. Expansion insures your capital from market volatility while also potentially seizing educational possibilities.

Consider a mix of growth and pay ventures:

As you near retirement, consider adjusting your investment strategy to strike a balance between growth and pay ventures. While growth-oriented resources such as equities can provide higher yields, income-producing initiatives such as securities, profit-paying stocks, or annuities can generate consistent revenue streams to help with retirement needs.

Handle your gambling openness:

As retirement approaches, it is critical to mitigate risk and protect your accumulated wealth. Consider gradually decreasing your openness to extremely risky initiatives and shifting your focus to more conservative options. Regardless, striking a balance between risk and reward is critical to ensuring your assumptions continue to grow while remaining steady.

Examine annuities and dependable pay options:

Annuities can provide a steady income stream during retirement. Examine several types of annuities, for example, immediate annuities or conceded pay annuities, and consider whether they align with your retirement aspirations. Consult with a financial advisor to determine the benefits and drawbacks of annuities and whether they are appropriate for your needs.

Audit and adjust your portfolio on a regular basis:

Examine your investment portfolio on a regular basis to ensure it is aligned with your retirement objectives and risk tolerance. Rebalance your portfolio on a regular basis to maintain your desired resource allocation. As you get closer to retirement, you'll definitely need to gradually shift toward a more secure investment strategy to protect your wealth and reduce market volatility.

Plan for medical expenses:

Medical care bills can be a significant burden in retirement. Consider the potential costs of clinical care, long-term care, and protection inclusion. Examine options such as government medical care and additional protection to reduce medical-related financial stress. Include medical care costs in your retirement budget to ensure that your investments can pay these expenses.

Seek professional advice:

Retirement planning can be complicated, so seeking advice from a professional financial advisor is essential. A financial advisor can assist you in researching investment options, determining your retirement needs, and developing a personalized retirement plan. Look for advisers who are experts in retirement planning and who have a trustee commitment to operate in your best interests.

Contributing to the brilliant years necessitates a well-thought-out point of view and a properly tested strategy. You can build a strong financial foundation that supports a pleasant and rewarding retirement by starting early, growing your endeavors, managing risk, and seeking expert counsel. Regularly survey and

To stay focused and take advantage of your retirement reserve cash, adjust your speculation technique based on the situation.

10

The Board of Directors and Resource Security

Systems of Support

Supporting systems put executives' approaches used by financial backers and organizations to protect against potential losses or antagonistic developments in the financial business sectors at risk. These techniques are intended to counterbalance or mitigate the impact of price fluctuations, unpredictability, or other risks associated with speculation.

Financial backers' support mechanisms include:

Agreements of Fate:

Prospective contracts are agreements to exchange a resource at a predetermined price on a specific future date. Financial backers can use fates agreements to protect against price increases in products, monetary standards, or financial instruments. Financial backers might protect themselves from prospective losses caused by unfavorable cost developments by holding a counterbalancing position to their current property.

Choices:

Choices grant the right, but not the obligation, to trade a resource at a predetermined cost within a specified time frame. Financial supporters can use options to hedge against downside risk by purchasing put options, which increase in value as the price of the concealed resource falls. Call options can also be used to protect against predicted losses in short positions or to protect against missed potential gain opportunities.

Forward Contracts:

Forward agreements, like prospect contracts, are deals to trade a resource at a predetermined cost on a specific future date. However, unlike destiny contracts placed on trades, forward agreements are rewritten and exchanged directly between parties. Forward agreements can be used to protect against cash conversion standard fluctuations or to lock in item costs.

Expansion:

Spreading endeavors across numerous resource classes, businesses, or geological regions is a commonly used supporting tactic. Financial backers attempt to reduce their exposure to explicit risks associated with individual enterprises by diversifying their holdings. In the case that one venture fails to work well, the losses may be offset by gains in other areas.

Selling on the cheap:

Short selling is a system in which financial supporters pur-chase pieces of a company and sell them with the expectation that the stock's price will fall. If the cost falls, the financial supporter can repurchase the offers at a reduced cost, return them to the lender, and profit from the difference. Short selling can act as a hedge against falling markets or specific stocks in a portfolio.

Supporting with Subsidiaries:

Subordinates, such as trades and collars, can be used to provide support. A financing cost trade, for example, can help a borrower protect against fluctuating loan fees, whereas a collar involves combining the acquisition of a put option and the offer of a call option to limit both potential gain and disadvantage gambles.

Portfolio Security:

Portfolio protection is a supplementary method that aims to protect the value of a speculative portfolio during times of market decline. It frequently incorporates the use of options or prospective agreements to limit potential losses. Financial back ers can naturally auction their holdings assuming that specific value boundaries are penetrated by setting out predetermined leave focuses or stop-misfortune instructions.

Normal Barriers:

Several companies typically support their risks through their tasks. For example, a carrier may enter into long-distance fuel contracts to hedge against fluctuations in oil prices, or a company with global operations may mitigate cash risk by conducting business in the local currencies of the countries in which it operates.

It's crucial to remember that while risk-reduction measures might help, they also come with associated costs and expected restrictions. Supporting does not always provide complete security or unexpected returns. Before implementing any supporting systems, investors should thoroughly assess their risk tolerance, financial objectives, and consult with professionals.

Protection:

Keeping Your Speculations Safe

Protection is a critical tool for preserving your speculations and managing risk. Whether you're an entrepreneur or a sole financial backer, protection can help you defend your assets and provide financial security if unwanted events occur. Here are a few various methods protection can help you protect your ventures:

Property safeguarding:

Property insurance protects physical assets like as structures, hardware, and inventory from damage caused by catastrophes such as fire, burglary, or natural disasters. This type of insurance can help to secure your business or personal property by providing monetary compensation to repair or replace damaged property.

Obligation Defense:

Risk insurance protects against cases of carelessness, errors, or other incidents that result in serious injury or property damage to others. This type of insurance can help to protect your investments by paying lawful expenses, settlements, or rulings that arise from such cases.

Life insurance:

Life insurance provides financial security to your friends and family in the event of your untimely death. It can also help to protect your ventures by providing assets to satisfy any outstanding commitments or fees and ensuring that your recipients are taken care of.

Handicap Security:

Incapacity insurance provides revenue replacement in the event of a disability that prevents you from working. This type of insurance can help protect your business by ensuring that you can continue to meet your financial obligations even if you are unable to work.

Long-term Care Security:

Long-term care insurance provides financial assistance for medical expenses associated with aging or chronic disease. This type of insurance can help to protect your investments by providing assets to cover the costs of long haul care, such as nursing homes, home medical services, or assisted living.

Digital Security:

Digital protection provides assurance against digital threats such as data breaches, digital assaults, and other digital-related incidents. This type of security can help to protect your business by covering the price of data recovery, legal fees, and other expenditures associated with a digital attack.

Protection for Chiefs and Officials:

Protection for chiefs and officials protects those filling in as chiefs or officials of an organization from incidents of careless-ness, blunders, or oversights in their responsibilities. This type of insurance can help to protect your investments by paying legal fees and settlements associated with such instances.

Umbrella coverage:

Umbrella protection extends liability coverage beyond the limitations of your previous protection contracts. This type of insurance can help to protect your business by providing additional financial protection in the event of a catastrophic event that exceeds the coverage limits of your other contracts.

Overall, security is an important tool for preserving your specu-lations and managing risk. By comprehending your protection alternatives and selecting the best inclusion for your require-ments, you can help ensure that your speculations are safe from unforeseen events and achieve monetary security.

Domain Arrangement:

Domain planning is an important interaction that includes managing and organizing your resources to ensure the seamless exchange of wealth and the fulfillment of your wishes after your death. You can get your heritage and provide financial security to your relatives and family by participating in smart domain planning. Here are some important factors to consider while planning a bequest:

Confirmation and Will:
 A will is a legally binding document that expresses your wishes about the distribution of your assets after your death. It allows you to appoint receivers, choose an agent to handle your domain, and possibly select gatekeepers for minor children. Drafting a will is critical for ensuring that your resources are conveyed by your preferences and limiting the possibility of disagreements.

Trusts:
 Trusts are versatile legal structures that can assist manage and distribute resources while potentially lowering domain fees. They allow you to transfer resources to a legal administrator who will keep and manage them on your behalf. Trusts can provide benefits such as security, resource assurance, and the ability to specify conditions for resource appropriation.

General legal authority:
 A legal authority is a legally binding document that empowers someone to make financial and legal decisions on your behalf if you become incapacitated. By appointing a trusted individual as your full legal authority, you ensure that your financial affairs will be properly managed if you are unable to make decisions for yourself.

Mandatory medical care:
 Medical services directives, such as a living will or medical

care legal authority, allow you to express your preferences for clinical therapy and end-of-life decisions. If you are unable to convey your desires, these records provide guidance to your friends and family as well as clinical specialists. Medical care orders ensure that your wishes are met and alleviate the strain on your friends and family during difficult times.

Assignments to Recipients:

Survey and update recipient assignments on financial records, retirement plans, additional security strategies, and other resources. Ensure that your tasks are up to date and in line with your overall bequest planning objectives. Consider contingency beneficiaries in the event that your essential recipients are unable to obtain the resources.

Keeping Household Expenses to a Minimum:

Investigate strategies to decrease bequest charges with the assistance of an experienced domain arranging lawyer or financial advisor. Giving resources during your lifetime, establishing irrevocable life covering trusts, or making generous contributions can all help to reduce the taxation rate on your property and expand the resources available to your recipients.

Arranging Business Progression:

If you own a business, develop a comprehensive succession plan to ensure a smooth transfer of ownership and executives. Distinguish possible successors, describe their positions and responsibilities, and establish processes to limit interruptions to business tasks while they are in action.

Regular Surveys and Updates

Bequest planning is not a one-time occurrence. It is critical to review and update your bequest plan on a regular basis or when major life events occur, such as marriage, divorce, the birth of children or grandchildren, or changes in financial circumstances. Regular auditing ensures that your home arrangement is current and in line with your expectations.

Look for Effective Direction:

Domain arranging may be confusing, so enlisting the assistance of experts, for example, house arranging lawyers, monetary advisors, and duty experts, is strongly advised. They may help you navigate the legal and financial intricacies, ensure compliance with relevant legislation, and provide critical guidance based on your specific circumstances.

Give and teach:

Examine your house arrangement openly with your friends and family, recipients, and essential people involved in its execution. Enlighten them on your ambitions, the location of essential archives, and the logic behind your decisions. Teach your relatives about the domain arranging procedure so that they are better prepared to deal with your endeavors in accordance with your objectives.

You can get your legacy, protect your friends and family, and ensure the peaceful transition of your resources by engaging in detailed house preparation. Begin the cycle early, get professional advice, and periodically assess and update your domain plan to adapt to changing conditions and goals. Making these steps can bring inner peace and help to ensure that your domain is managed in accordance with your desires, carelessness, setbacks, or other incidents that result in major injury or property mischief to others. This type of protection can help to protect your theory by covering genuine costs, settlements, or decisions that arise from such situations.

Inclusion in daily life:

Life insurance provides financial security to your loved ones in the case of your unexpected death. It can also help to protect your endeavors by providing resources to meet any residual commitments or expenses and ensuring that your beneficiaries are maintained.

Handicap Safety:

Inadequacy insurance provides income replacement in the event of an impairment that prevents you from working. This type of security can assist you defend your endeavors by assuring that you can continue to accumulate your financial obligations even if you are unable to work.

Long-term Care Insurance:

Long-term care insurance provides financial support for therapeutic benefits costs associated with developing or maintaining sickness. This type of insurance can help you protect your hypotheses by providing resources to cover the costs of long-term care, such as nursing homes, home clinical services, or supported living.

Computerized Insurance:

Advanced security provides assurance against advanced risks

such as data breaches, advanced attacks, and other computer-related incidents. This type of insurance can assist you in defending your activities by covering the price of data recovery, legal fees, and other expenses associated with a digital attack.

Security for Bosses and Authorities:

Bosses and authorities assurance shields individuals serving as bosses or authorities of a company against instances of disregard, faults, or oversights in their responsibilities. This type of insurance helps protect your beliefs by covering genuine expenditures and settlements linked with such instances.

Umbrella coverage:

Umbrella security goes above and beyond the standards of your existing assurance policies to provide additional duty consideration. This type of insurance can help to protect your endeavors by providing more financial security in the event of an unfortunate incident that excels the inclusion farthest extent of your numerous plans.

Overall, assurance is an essential tool for safeguarding your theories and managing risk. You can assist ensure that your hypotheses are protected from unanticipated disasters and attain financial security by sorting out your insurance options and selecting the proper incorporation for your needs.

Organizing Your Space:

Area administration is a vital association that includes preparing and sorting out your assets to ensure the seamless exchange of wealth and the fulfillment of your desires after your death. You can leave a legacy and provide financial stability to your loved ones by engaging in smart space organization. The following are some basic elements to consider when estate planning:

Affirmation and Willpower:
A will is a formal document that expresses your desires for the distribution of your possessions after your death. It allows you to distribute beneficiaries, appoint an expert to govern your area, and even choose guardians for minor children. Drafting a will is critical for ensuring that your assets are conveyed by your desires and limiting the possibility of disagreements.

Trusts:
Trusts are adaptable authentic alternatives that can assist manage and distribute assets while potentially reducing space costs. They authorize you to transfer assets to a legal head who will retain and manage them for your beneficiaries. Trusts can provide benefits such as security, asset confirmation, and the capacity to show requirements for asset appointment.

General legal authority:
A legitimate authority is a legal document that gives someone the authority to make financial and genuine decisions on your behalf in the event that you become incapacitated. By choosing a trusted individual as your entire legal authority, you assure that your financial endeavors will be properly managed if you are unable to make decisions for yourself.

Clinical consideration commands, such as a living will or clinical consideration lawful power, allow you to express your desires on clinical treatment and end-of-life decisions. These documents provide direction to your loved ones and therapeutic specialists in the event that you are unable to communicate your tendencies. Clinical consideration orders ensure that your desires are followed and that the burden of dynamic on your loved ones is reduced at trying times.

Beneficial Jobs:

Examine and update beneficiary responsibilities for financial records, retirement plans, additional security draws near, and varied assets. Ensure that your tasks are up to date and in line with your general endowment organization goals. If your primary beneficiaries are unable to obtain the assets, consider contingent beneficiaries.

Limiting Home Costs:

Consult a seasoned area organizing attorney or financial advisor to investigate strategies to limit endowment charges. Giving assets throughout your lifetime, distributing irrevocable life inclusion trusts, or employing charitable donations, for example, can help with lowering the tax assessment rate on your property and increasing the assets accessible to your beneficiaries.

Organizing a Business Movement:

If you operate a business, establish a complete movement to ensure a seamless difference between the chiefs and under lock and key. Recognize potential substitutions, depict their roles and responsibilities, and explore methodology to limit interferences with business assignments during progress.

Typical research and updates:
Inheritance planning is not a one-time occurrence. It is critical to review and revise your estate plan on a regular basis or when major life changing events occur, such as marriage, divorce, the presenting of children or grandkids, or changes in financial circumstances. Conventional assessment ensures that your house course of action is up to date and in accordance with your assumptions.

Look for Capable Course:
Space planning may be perplexing, so enlisting the help of specialists, for example, house organizing legal advisors, financial advisors, and obligation specialists, is strongly advised. They may assist you in investigating the genuine and financial complexities, ensuring compliance with statutory rules, and providing substantial assistance based on your individual situations.

Provide and Educate:
Examine your house plan with your loved ones, beneficiaries, and important persons involved in its execution. Inform them about your desires, the area of large papers, and the reasoning behind your decisions. Display the space coordinating method to your family members so that they are better equipped and ready to handle your endeavors as represented by your points.

You can receive your legacy, protect your loved ones, and ensure the seamless difference in your assets by engaging in comprehensive home arrangement. Begin the cycle early, seek qualified counsel, and analyze and update your area mean on a regular basis to adapt to changing conditions and objectives. Taking these actions will provide inward consistency and aid in ensuring that your region is dealt with in accordance with your desires.

Put resources into your understanding:

Contributing is a never-ending learning experience. Keep up to date on financial trends, industry advancements, and new venture valuable opportunities. Read financial news, follow reputable speculation sources, and consider expanding your knowledge through books, courses, and classes.

If required, seek competent exhortation:

If you are unsure about your investment selections or require guidance, try speaking with a financial advisor that specializes in long haul money management. They can provide tailored advice based on your financial situation, risk tolerance, and long run aspirations.

In summary, contributing for the long haul entails identifying clear objectives, maintaining a long-term mindset, diversifying your portfolio, focusing on quality resources, and remaining trained during market shifts. By adhering to these guidelines, you can increase your chances of achieving your long-term financial objectives and creating financial security.

Investigating the Business Sector

Exploring the market can be a difficult task because it requires understanding business sector elements, making informed decisions, and adapting to changing conditions. Whether you are a novice or a seasoned financial backer,

Consider the following factors as you continue your market research:

Conduct thorough investigation:

Prior to entering the market, it is critical to conduct a thorough investigation of the business opportunities you are considering. This includes analyzing budget summaries, comprehending industry trends, evaluating competition, and staying current on relevant news and events. Research supports you in making informed decisions based on solid evidence.

Describe your method of speculation:

A fair venture strategy is essential for market exploration. Determine your risk tolerance, time frame, and financial objectives. Determine whether you need to concentrate on long haul effective money management, esteem effective money management, development contributing, or a combination of systems. Your procedure will guide your business decisions and keep you on track in the face of market shifts.

Make an enlarged portfolio:

Enhancement is a risk management process that entails spreading your bets over numerous resource classes, areas, and geographic locations. By diversifying your portfolio, you can mitigate the impact of any particular speculation's poor performance and potentially boost results. Examine and adjust your portfolio on a regular basis to ensure it is in accordance with your risk tolerance and business objectives.

Keep up to date:

Keep up to date on market trends, monetary indicators, and relevant news that may effect your guesses. Examine monetary distributions, adhere to legitimate sources, and explore using monetary apparatuses and stages that provide consistent market data. The more knowledgeable you are, the better prepared you will be to make decisions in a volatile market environment.

Handle your emotions:

Feelings can frequently cause irrational business decisions. It's critical to deal with your emotions, especially during times of market volatility. Try not to make rash decisions out of fear or covetousness. Stick to your investment strategy, focus on the long haul, and avoid being swayed by short-term market fluctuations.

Risk assessment and adjustment:

Screen and analyze the risk associated with your speculations on a regular basis. Learn about market instability, administrative changes, international threats, and macroeconomic conditions. Maintain flexibility and change your speculation strategy as needed. Economic realities may need changes to your portfolio or investment strategy from time to time in order to better align with changing conditions.

Profit from mistakes:

Contributing includes risks, and making mistakes along the way is normal. Use any enterprise failures as opportunities to learn and grow your dynamic cycle. Examine what went wrong, distinguish illustrations, and adjust your process as needed. Remember that contributing is a never-ending learning experience, and that experience may be a valuable teacher.

If required, seek competent exhortation:

If you are feeling overwhelmed or want expertise in specific areas of efficient financial planning, consider seeking professional assistance. Monetary advisors can provide tailored advice based on your specific needs and goals. They can help you investigate difficult speculation items, provide insights into market patterns, and assist with portfolio management.

Keep in mind that efficiently investigating the market necessitates a combination of knowledge, discipline, and adaptability. By directing research, characterizing your methodology, improving your portfolio, staying informed, dealing with emotions, observing risk, learning from mistakes, and seeking professional advice when necessary, you can explore the market with more certainty and increase your chances of meeting your financial objectives.

11

Conclusion

Readers of "Money Seed of Happiness: Cultivating Financial Independence and Abundance for a Happy Retirement" find themselves on the verge of a profound transformation.

Dr. Bob Kenneth has expertly walked us through the complex garden of personal finance, cultivating our grasp of wealth creation and retirement planning. As we near the end of this literary voyage, the fruits of our labor are ripe for the picking.

Dr. Bob Kenneth has beautifully explored the relationships between financial independence, plenty, and pleasure throughout the book. It's not just about acquiring wealth for the sake of amassing wealth; it's about using it as a tool to construct a life of fulfillment and meaning. This sophisticated point of view distinguishes the book from others in the personal finance genre, emphasizing the comprehensive character of a wealthy retirement.

The final chapters serve as a call to action, encouraging readers to use what they've learned in their own lives. Dr. Bob Kenneth encourages us to plant the seed of change here, whether it's assessing our financial goals, altering our investment strategy, or reevaluating our spending patterns. This book presents readers with step-by-step instructions to help them embark on this revolutionary journey.

Furthermore, Dr.Bob Kenneth is not afraid to touch the emotional components of retirement preparation. The move to retirement is a huge life event, and the book provides helpful suggestions on how to traverse the emotional terrain that typically goes along with it. The value of a well-rounded, meaningful retirement is not lost in the financial specifics; it is inextricably linked to them.

We say goodbye to the pages of "Money Seed of Happiness" with a renewed sense of financial empowerment and clarity. Dr. Bob Kenneth's knowledge seed have taken root in our minds, and we are better prepared to tackle the difficulties and opportunities that lie ahead.

Finally, "Money Seed of Happiness" is more than simply a book; it's a road map to a better financial future and a happier retirement. It's an invitation to take care of our finances, create abundance, and reap the benefits of a happy retirement. We can now confidently embark on our own journeys toward financial freedom, affluence, and, ultimately, enduring happiness in retirement, having received wisdom from this wonderful literary voyage.

www.ingramcontent.com/pod-product-compliance
Lightning Source LLC
Chambersburg PA
CBHW062321290526
45794CB00005B/1843